What's My Childhood Got to Do With It?

HOW DISCOVERING YOUR PAST WILL BENEFIT YOUR FUTURE

What's My Childhood Got to Do With It?

Ainsley Grace Collins, LPC

Copyright © 2014 by Ainsley Grace Collins

Triple C Publishing, New River, Arizona

All rights reserved. No part of this publication may be reproduced, stored in a retrieval system, or transmitted in any form or by any means, electronic, mechanical, photocopying, recording, or otherwise without prior written permission. For copyright information, please contact the author at www.childhoodpower.com.

Permission to use quote on page 105 by Isabel Briggs Myers from *Gifts Differing: Understanding Personality Type* by Isabel Briggs Myers (with Peter B. Myers) granted by CCP Inc.

Permission to use song lyrics on page 135 granted by Stacy Labriola, lyricist, MotherLode Trio, *Watching You Go*.

Permission to use quote on page 147 by Steven C. Kalas granted by Steven C. Kalas.

Excerpt from *Rush Hour* on page 184 granted courtesy of New Line Productions, Inc.

Printed in the United States.

Please note this book is intended to educate individuals on topics related to self-discovery and is not a substitute for mental health treatment. The reader should consult a mental health professional in matters requiring specialized attention.

Although the author has made every effort to ensure that the information in this book was correct at press time, the author does not assume and hereby disclaim any liability to any party for any loss, damage, or disruption caused by errors or omissions, whether such errors or omissions result from negligence, accident, or any other cause.

The author has recreated events, locales, and conversations from memory. In order to maintain anonymity in certain cases, the names of individuals and places have been changed. Some names and identifying details have been changed to protect the privacy of individuals.

ISBN: 978-0-9882008-0-7 (Hard Cover Edition)

ISBN: 978-0-9882008-1-4 (Soft Cover Edition)

ISBN: 978-0-9882008-2-1 (ebook)

To my sons, Gabriel and Zachary,

the spurs behind my journey

Acknowledgements

I believe few goals in life materialize alone. This book is no different. I have been fortunate to have some special people in my life whose belief *in* and support *of* me has made an immeasurable difference.

Appreciation goes to Dave Curtis, Tom and Valerie Erhard, Dr. Cynthia Hoard, Craig Howard, Brad Hudson, Andy Kohlhepp, Renee Kramb, Scott Mielke, Dr. Elsie Moore, Liz Mulder, Frank Newton, Mary Oliver, Rich Parker, Lourdes Pessetto, Doug Pullin, Chris Reed, Joan Shaffer, "Dispatch" Dave Scott, Becky Simmons, Misty Standage, Carmen Westberg, Rea Wharton, and the late Dana Campbell, Tom Ferguson, Gertrude Howard, and Holly Marino. Each of you have added value to my life.

For their enduring devotion, snuggles go to Fred, Kenai, Maxine, Punk, Maggie-Moo, and grand dogs Bart and Vegas. You demonstrate beyond a doubt why you are *man's best friend*. To Blaze and Cowboy – your beauty outside my office window grazing in the pasture inspires me beyond words. And to Swede and Abbers, although you were taken far too early, your spirits are with me every day as I remember the splendor of your existence.

For their invaluable talent and professionalism, I want to thank my cover designer, George Foster, my interior designer, Deborah Perdue, and my editor, Mike Sirota. You made this challenging endeavor a joy, and I learned enormous amounts from each of you. To my pre-content team of Anastasia Collins, Janessa Hernandez, and Kristin Walker, your time and feedback set the course for this book. Thank you for your courage, input, and support.

My appreciation would not be complete without mentioning my hundreds of patients over the years who have allowed me the privilege of being a part of their lives. Your stories validate the reason I wrote this book.

Special gratitude goes to:

    Brian Collins, the father of my children,
    Jody Womack, my fellow psychoanalyst, confidant, and friend,
    Lynn Anderson, for being *you* and encouraging me to be *me*,
    Sky Carver, for a kindness that changed the course of my life, and
    Teresa "Tess" Johnson-Vanney, my endearing and treasured friend for over forty years (are we really that old?) through both joy and heartache.

And to Steven C. Kalas and Dr. Frederick C. Green, Jr. – your commitment to humanness gave me the richest gift possible: my wholeness.

Lastly, I thank my sons, Gabriel Jacob and Zachary Luke. Being your mother is the greatest honor imaginable.

Table of Contents

Introduction i

Chapter One 1
Mama, Don't Let Your Babies Grow Up to Be *Normal*
Normal Versus Healthy

Chapter Two 17
By the Time I Get to My Emotions
Roadblocks to the Past

Chapter Three 31
Ticket to Change
Tools to Grow By

Chapter Four 47
You Messed Up My Life
Healthy, Dysfunctional, and Abusive

Chapter Five 63
Great Balls of Energy
Acting Out – Looking Inward

Chapter Six 77
Growing Up is Hard to Do
Attachment and Development

Chapter Seven 93
The Greatest Organ of All
Personality or Temperament

Chapter Eight 109
Born to Be Me
Defense Mechanisms and Resiliency

Chapter Nine 125
Growing Up is Hard to Do, the Sequel
Individuation and the Familial Plight

Chapter Ten 143
I Left My Heart in Yesterday
Grief and the Discovery of Loss

Chapter Eleven 157
Oops, I Messed Up Again
The Lost Art of Solving Problems

Chapter Twelve 175
I Only Have Words for You
It's All About the Communication

Chapter Thirteen 191
Stairway to Freedom
Victims, Blame, and Forgiveness

Chapter Fourteen 211
Can't Buy Me Peace
Change and the Pursuit of Therapy

Chapter Fifteen 227
Sweet Home, Authenticity
Reality and Choices

Epilogue 241

Additional Reading 243

Exercises 245

Do not be afraid of the past.

If people tell you it is irrevocable,

do not believe them.

– Oscar Wilde

Introduction

Each time I crouched behind the driver's seat of our aging Fiat, I whispered in hopes someone would hear me, "Please don't make me come back here again." But day after day my father used me to escape our house, fueling my mother's inquiry into his secretive behavior.

"She wants some candy," my father pointed, insinuating me. He then quickened us out the door before my mother thought to impede his action.

Sometimes we went to Pearson's, our neighborhood market, where I bought my favorite one-cent licorice sticks or red coins, two for a penny. Other times my father bypassed this formality and drove directly to his destination. Though disappointed, I dared not question him.

Our excursions took us to one of three buildings, each bearing a similarity except in color. Honing the logic of a four year old, I named them 'the red office', 'the white office', and 'the black office', and an internal guessing game resulted each outing to see which we would visit.

Faint and barely audible in contrast to the car door slamming, my father's "I'll be just a few minutes" enforced the doubtfulness of his words. This was my cue to climb behind the driver's seat and hide under a black horse blanket, my portable security that rarely left my side. Intermittently I'd press my face against the window and spy on the men coming and going from the structure, praying my father was one of the silhouettes visible under the dim parking lot lights before I was discovered, kidnapped, and tortured.

When we arrived home, my mother glared at my father and me as though she was a drill sergeant inspecting her troops. "What took you so long?" resonated to neither of us in particular, though quickly commanded intimidation. "Did you really go just to Pearson's?" Knowing my father would remain silent, the fear of betrayal induced my legs to unscramble enough to run toward the safety beneath my bed, my now common destination when in anguish.

With age, an awareness of my father's reckless driving practices obliged me to supervise our safety. When flashing lights trumped my pleas for him to stay in his lane, however, I instinctively crawled to my hiding place and monitored the officer as he handcuffed my father and escorted him away, confiscating the gun found shielded between the seat cushions. When the coast was clear, I ran home to the emptiness of our house, neither the incident nor my presence there ever acknowledged.

Shortly thereafter, my father stopped making up stories in order to get out of the house. Leaving and returning in silence, I guess he grew either accepting of or oblivious to looks of condemnation. Otherwise, nothing changed. If at home, it was a sure bet you would find him by the back door leaning on the kitchen counter between a burning cigarette and a disguised drink.

As for me, I guess I should have been happy. Never again did my father solicit me for his outings. But the truth was, I was no longer needed. In the realm of my father's life, I had become obsolete.

Obsolete
Written in therapy, 1993

INTRODUCTION

Inevitably, we all have a childhood story. Some are happy, some are sad, and others remain undefined. When understood, our stories allow us to discover our true selves – our authenticity. In turn, we gain power. Every childhood has truths hidden in its depths eager for acknowledgement, if permitted. To help show the implications of one's childhood, each chapter of this book begins with a segment from my past. Although my story may be more or less complex than yours, the process of self-discovery differs little, and it is my hope that through joining in my journey you will be able to recognize how understanding your first eighteen years will enhance the rest of your life.

So, *what's your childhood got to do with it?* More than you might realize. Why not find out?

Chapter One

Mama, Don't Let Your Babies Grow Up to Be *Normal*

Normal Versus Healthy

Unlike most little girls, I never wanted to be a princess. My dream was to live in the 1800s, get up with the sun, feed the chickens, milk the cows, then jump on my horse and gallop off to the little schoolhouse, if only so I could ride home again in the afternoon. This, however, would not be my destiny. Instead, I was born into a Swedish middle-class family in a small redneck town in the rainy northwest, the lumber industry steering our community's economy like a seesaw. Logging accidents killed more people I knew than did natural causes, and not until I was about ten did the first Black family move to our area. People walked up to them and asked if they could touch their skin. This family's appearance disturbed my fundamentalist grandparents, though I was not surprised given their refusal to buy any Japanese-made products since World War II. Although not fully understanding the concept of discrimination, I figured it best to keep my kissing the neighboring Cherokee boy a secret.

Our last name was familiar in our town due to my grandmother teaching piano lessons and my grandfather composing music and conducting Handel's *Messiah*. After touring in Europe, my grandparents gave my father the middle name *Ducret* after a French symphony associate, perhaps in hopes that their only child would become a musical protégé. This did not happen, though sometimes I lied and told people my father was a concert pianist, if for no other reason than to feel proud about something. When that got old, I simply told them he was dead. This seemed easier than trying to explain what I didn't understand. Never discussed in our family was what was wrong with my father, and I lacked the courage to ask.

The author as a baby

Though not a place I considered welcoming, my mandatory piano lessons demanded weekly visits to my grandparents' home. Covered with thick plastic, their furniture screamed "off limits", a message echoed by the rest of the décor obviously not purchased with children in mind. Adorned with countless bookshelves, their living room created the facade of a library rather than gathering place, and while otherwise drab, one's attention could not help but wander to the full-fledged telephone booth that sat conspicuously across from their console television. Although an enticing play area, I somehow knew any indulgence was a forbidden pleasure. My only fear greater than receiving a reprimand from my grandparents was them asking whether I went *number one* or *number two* upon my completion of using their

CHAPTER ONE

bathroom. Why this mattered I was unclear, but I attempted to avoid the situation at all costs, including almost wetting my pants. Near the end of my grandfather's life as I was entering adulthood, I was able to see a glimmer of his sense of humor that had not been evident to me as a young child. My grandmother, however, who lived another twenty-five years to the age of 109, continued to be a reminder of my shortcomings through her once-piercing words, "Why can't you be bubbly and happy like your sister?"

While I don't remember the exact moment I learned of my father's disappointment at my being born a third girl, I know I attempted to prove my worthiness to him from that point forward. This task dominated my world and set the stage for the bulk of my memories. One of my earliest quests for approval began around the age of four when I took stamps from his closet and stuck them onto envelopes in order to *help* him while he showered. Obviously lacking was my grasp of stamp collecting and the value of slobbered-on stamps. When my father walked in and saw me, he said nothing. I did not fear that my father would yell or hit me; my torment stemmed from his silence. No matter what I did, my father appeared indifferent, motivating me to gain a more comprehendible response. For the next ten years, I did just that, escalating my once innocent attention-seeking gestures of playing with his stamps and hiding his socks to stealing money from his wallet and, eventually, attempting to kill myself.

Equal to my determination to gain my father's attention was my mother's preoccupation with my older sisters. Close in age and nearly inseparable, they seemed to relate to our mother with an

The author at about two years old

The author at about four years old

ease that I envied. Perhaps meaning to compensate for what my father lacked in the parenting arena, I found her strictness and perfectionism unwelcoming, a feeling that aided in holding our bond hostage. I have little doubt she tried her best in what appeared to be a lopsided battle against her, but as a young child I was absent of such insight and it was only the here and now that created my experiences. In the end, I gave up defending myself in our chronic disconnect somewhere around the age of thirteen. Not long thereafter, it felt as though she gave up on me as well.

Feeling as if an outsider much of the time, I found comfort in our four-legged family member, Michael Bosco, an Irish setter. From the time he licked my face after knocking me over with the swish of his irrepressible tail when I was a toddler, we rarely parted company. If not with me, it was because I had to leave him behind when told to go with my sisters to their friends' homes, an unfortunate consequence of living in a neighborhood devoid of children my own age and a mother who didn't seem to want me underfoot. I acquired the label of *tag-along,* and practical jokes soon followed. I can still hear my sisters and their friends giggle when I realized that blood was red and not blue as they showed me when pointing to my veins. Weary of being humiliated, I practiced becoming invisible like my favorite cartoon character, Casper the Ghost, and before long my skill at hiding in silence edged proficiency. I like to think my talent at this new endeavor is what permitted me to go unnoticed in the midst of grown-up conversation. More likely, however, was that no one cared I was privy to information far too complex for my young mind to comprehend. Perhaps my sisters fared better by having

CHAPTER ONE

The author at about nine years old with Michael Bosco

each other to sort through the contradictions of our environment, but I felt alone in the turmoil, as if deserted on a battlefield unable to distinguish between friendly and enemy fire.

To curb my loneliness, I embarked upon the art of daydreaming, and my love of horses played well into my magical world of make-believe. By simply closing my eyes, I envisioned a place where I could have my three favorite things: horses, dogs, and macaroni and cheese. And when my fantasies were not enough, my love affair with the Old West prompted me to put on my cowboy outfit complete with holster and guns or my Indian get-up with a feather headdress. Ditching my shirt and baring my chest to impersonate the warriors seen on television was perhaps also an appeal to be the boy my father wanted. I vaguely remember something about war paint, but won't confess to any such gesture. Scouting the neighborhood for a boy who sometimes rode his horse in sight of our house, I ran for blocks one day crazed with both fear and excitement in order to catch up to him. Incredibly shy, though curiously mimicking a miniature John Wayne, I kept my distance hoping when he saw me he would stop and ask if I wanted to ride his horse. I was positive my life depended on it. But after what seemed miles without any indication of acknowledgement, I reluctantly conceded defeat as tears spilled down my face. His rejection served to reinforce all the insecurities I already had about myself, leaving me with only one belief: *I didn't matter.*

We lived in only one house as a family and I would be its last occupant, moving out at the age of nineteen. By then, no emotion lingered, and years passed before my buried disdain materialized in the form of haunting memories.

"You're weird."
"No I'm not."
"Yes you are."
"No I'm not."
"Yes you are."

Oh, the bickering of children; standing their ground, not wanting to be different.

Normalcy is an important concept to us. We don't like when people call us odd, unusual, weird, or peculiar. This begins when we are young. As children, we assume sameness. We take for granted that other families mimic ours. If we have cereal for breakfast, we believe others do also. If mom tucks us into bed and reads us a story each evening, we think other children have the same bedtime routine. Our level of development and limited experiences mold us. We also presume something else: we think our life is *normal,* that *we* are normal. And from these early perceptions we begin defining our place in the world.

Though we don't always recognize them as such, we take many of

CHAPTER ONE

our childhood beliefs with us into adulthood. Engrained in us through repetition, familiarity, and influence, these beliefs stem from our environment and culture. In the end, whether or not these beliefs endure or deteriorate is dependent on one's unique temperament and developing personality. The beliefs we adopt then make up how we view the world, and it is from this *worldview* that we base our behaviors and decision-making. If you are like most people, some of your behaviors and decisions contribute to the disappointments in your life. This fact founds the purpose of exploring your past: to understand why you do what you do so that you have the opportunity to expand what *is* effective and improve what *isn't*.

Consider the little girl who grew up watching her father hit her mother. She, in turn, married a man who hit her. In time, her husband nearly killed her, the police came, Child Protective Services took their children, her husband went to prison, and she ended up homeless. This is an example of how one's worldview based on the perception of *normalcy* in childhood results in tragedy. When you take the time to understand your past and gain a healthy perspective of your experiences, you are less apt to make decisions that cost you valuable assets such as time, relationships, money, and health. All it takes is a willingness to learn. I like to think of it this way: *Sometimes what we most need to see is invisible.*

Pretend you are five years old. Life is pretty cool. You're pretty cool. There is no doubt in your mind you are *normal*. When you get to kindergarten, however, you discover something: differences. Not all the children are like you. One boy is speaking a language you don't understand. Another boy has blue streaks in his hair. Then a loud and obnoxious girl appears. You feel uncomfortable. Your worldview does not include these observations. As a result, another concept forms in your mind: *abnormality*. Soon, the bickering begins.

"You're weird."

"No I'm not."

"Yes you are."

"No I'm not."

"Yes you are."

Normal is one of those subjective words in our language that has more than one meaning. In most cases, we use the word *normal* when we mean *usual* or *common,* as in "when do you normally eat dinner?" We even joke about the fact that if you are not *normal* then you must be *crazy*. Thus, the word *normal* presupposes an *okay-ness*. While on the surface this makes sense, this type of logic can also deceive us. What does *normal* really tell us? Consider my outings with my father. Were they *normal*? Yes, in the sense they were *usual* or *common* occurrences. But were they *okay*? And this is where an alternative definition of *normal* is helpful: *healthy*. Leaving a four-year-old child in a car unsupervised in a bar parking lot at night for hours and then driving home impaired probably doesn't equate *okay* for most responsible adults. Sometimes, then, what is *normal* can be contrary to what is *okay* or *healthy*. The reason why it is important to look at both definitions is because oftentimes, particularly as children, our perspective is limited to familiarity rather than what might be in our best interest. You've probably heard the parental plea of exaggeration when it comes to teenage reasoning, "So, if all your friends were going to jump off a cliff, would you jump too?" *Normal* is often a powerful influence, though not always the healthiest option.

Warning: as you begin this book, you might be tempted to take immediate action. My advice is to consider this book as you would a manual for a new product that states, "Read all instructions before using". In other words, reading and completing the exercises in this book are recommended first. I know, I don't like instructions either. I'm more the *try to figure it out* type of person. But sometimes that doesn't work well. Imagine going skydiving for the first time. I don't know about you, but I'm pretty sure I'd want to read all the directions on my parachute before jumping out of a plane at 12,000 feet. For the most favorable outcome, I offer the same advice to you regarding this book: read before you leap. Two crucial steps in this process are information gathering and gaining self-knowledge. When this is completed, you will then be ready to take any further action that is needed.

The exercises in this book serve to both guide you and teach you skills to help you understand your childhood story. They are meant to be completed in order, although you will utilize some of the exercises more than once. Keep in mind that you will benefit most if you take your time to answer them completely and honestly. I found that making a timeline is helpful, labeling the bottom from birth to eighteen with plenty of room for notes. There is no right or wrong way to construct your timeline. I urge you, in fact, to use your creativity. The idea is to make the important aspects from your childhood visual so you can more easily make connections and gain understanding. From this point forward, I will refer to this venue for gathering information as your *timeline*. So, let's get started.

> *Exercise 1a: Take a moment and think about three or four words that describe your overall childhood experience and write them on your timeline. This is your first step to achieving a healthier and more fulfilling life.*

I look at childhood as a puzzle that requires a variety of needs and information. When all these puzzle pieces are present and in their proper place, they make up the requirements for a healthy adult. More often than not during childhood some of these puzzle pieces become lost, damaged, or fail to materialize, creating a need in adulthood to go back and figure out what happened. Throughout this book you will learn what makes up these necessary puzzle pieces, how to identify when pieces are missing, damaged, or misplaced, and what to do when this occurs. As you complete your puzzle, your increase in self-awareness will promote a positive rippling effect, allowing your authentic self to emerge and empower you toward the life you desire.

As with any new endeavor, looking at your childhood may feel awkward at first, especially when facing experiences that cause you to feel vulnerable. I remember feeling resistant a number of times while in therapy and needing to remind myself that in order for positive results to materialize, I had to try. In time I realized the feelings of frustration, impatience, and fear are common when attempting something new. After a while, however, familiarity and competence take over, a process otherwise known as *the learning curve.* Even learning to ride a horse wasn't easy for me, but enduring a sore bottom and a bruised ego after falling off a few times proved beneficial in the end. Now, there is probably no place I feel more comfortable than on the back of a horse. Perhaps you can think about this adventure of discovering your childhood story as I do – as a trail ride where the untouched terrain provides an opportunity to look at life from a new perspective.

Exercise 1b: Close your eyes and envision your first memory. How old are you? Where are you? What are the circumstances? How is this memory significant to you? When you are finished with this memory, try to think of your second memory. Write these down on your timeline at the age they occurred.

The idea that most children do not question the *healthiness* of their lives is the basis for this book. Thus, the advantage of looking at your childhood from an adult perspective is that you now have a fully developed brain with which to analyze your past objectively. As a child, you lacked this ability. This means you are now able to differentiate between *normal* and *healthy,* an important aspect in understanding your childhood. Consider this: Although it is *normal* for many of us to sit in front of a computer much of the day, it is not particularly *healthy*. Studies have shown that weight gain, back problems, and poor circulation are consequences from sitting for long periods. The value of distinguishing between *normal* and *healthy* will become more evident in time. For now, it is simply important to know that both words are relevant to your success at understanding how your childhood shaped you, and that *healthy* is the desired goal.

Looking at my life from the outside, one might have thought my relationship with my father equated healthiness due to the amount of time we spent together. Although this seems like a reasonable conclusion, situations such as mine are why the phrase *quality time* was introduced some years back, referring to parents spending time with their children that is bonding rather than simply close in proximity. In truth, it felt as if my father only wanted me around when it benefitted him, like when he needed me as an excuse to get out of the house or when he wanted his feet tickled, an unpopular job due to the smell. In time I grew to question his love for me, especially because my requests for him to walk the dog, play catch, or take pictures with me were met with rejection. As a result, I learned to react cautiously and defensively toward him, and these behaviors continued throughout my childhood, further alienating us from each other.

Children learn behaviors from the experiences to which they are exposed. A mother who teaches her son to say *please* and *thank you* day after day to instill good manners is deliberately teaching a certain lesson. On the other hand, parents also teach their children behaviors unintentionally, as my father did by driving while intoxicated. I imagine some would say I grew to become every driver's worst nightmare: a proficient backseat driver with stiff body, teeth gritted, and foot pressing the floorboard. I am still unclear whether we ever hit anything. I *do* know in those days without required seatbelts that my small, thin frame slammed into the glove box more than once and that it took years for me to overcome my fear when getting into a car as a passenger. Regardless, I don't think this was something my father set out to teach me. By placing me in such a situation, however, my body responded logically to an unhealthy situation. Then, in time, my anxiety became a learned response any time I got into a car regardless of the danger it posed. What this shows is how a behavior in childhood thought to be *normal* can actually be *unhealthy* and cause stress in adulthood.

Even in the healthiest homes, children grow up learning unhealthy unintentional lessons. Parenting is just too imperfect of an art. Dysfunctional and abusive homes carry an even higher chance for undesirable outcomes. Along with feeling anxious, I also learned to withhold my feelings, pretend everything was fine when it wasn't, not ask questions, and lie in order to avoid conflict. These behaviors not only took me further from my true self and set the stage for my developing depression, but they also founded my primary response to stress: running away. What began as a way to avoid taking sides with either parent by hiding in my room, escalated over time to ending any situation I didn't want to deal with, whether that meant leaving a room, a job, or even a city. All these unintentional lessons became patterned responses, engraining them into my personality as I grew up. In my young developing mind, these learned behaviors felt *normal*. With little awareness as to their destructiveness, and with no one intervening to teach me healthier skills, these behaviors followed me into adulthood and remained a part of my identity until my life began to unravel and I felt forced to look inward.

As was the case in my life, unintentional lessons often remain hidden until something brings them to our awareness. Even then, we sometimes fail to question them or calculate their negative impact on our lives. We don't understand why a once-useful behavior or response from childhood no longer benefits us. Running away, for example, helped me to avoid confrontation with my parents, but it did not prove particularly beneficial in resolving situations in adulthood. Not until I understood where the behavior originated did I realize it was not an innate part of me. Having acquired numerous such behaviors, I began adulthood thinking I was an impulsive, secretive, anti-social, anxious, non-communicative, awkward, boring, sad, unpleasant, reactive, and scared person. And, as you can imagine, this didn't make me much fun to be around. I considered myself personality-less because of my unpredictable behaviors. Deep down, however, I felt someone had invaded my body and stolen the *true* me. It was this gut belief that nourished my quest for answers.

The adverse result of children learning unintentional lessons is they usually lack options. Children have little say in the quality of life they are born into and the experiences they encounter. Unfortunately, they routinely pay the consequences. Juvenile detention centers house many children who were simply reacting to or modeling the unhealthiness in their lives. Any venue can be negligent of a child's healthy emotional development, including extended family, neighbors, friends, schools, sport groups, clubs, and churches, substantiating the fact that raising children truly is a societal responsibility.

The odds that you grew up having avoided unhealthiness in your childhood are minimal. Consider thinking of your childhood as a buried treasure chest filled with valuables that can make you smarter, stronger, happier, and healthier. All you have to do is find them. Are you ready to look?

🌶. *Exercise 1c: How would you answer the question, "Who am I?" Begin by writing down six characteristics that define who you are right now. In other words, if you were writing a novel and you were the main character, how would you describe yourself so the reader would feel as though they know your personality? Because we are all human, try to think of three positive characteristics and three characteristics that you would like to improve upon.*

Discovering the source of your thoughts, beliefs, and behaviors from childhood is part of the puzzle I spoke about earlier. All the pieces to your authentic self await your discovery. The anxiety I felt as a passenger in a car was one of the more straightforward puzzle pieces I found when examining my past. After years of turning into a possessed woman when riding in a car, simply understanding the source of my anxiety helped to deplete some of the power behind my reaction. I'm not sure that was much consolation to my eldest son, however, who first had to endure me as a driving instructor.

Discovering your childhood is not about miraculously erasing any bad memories or changing history. Examining your past is about curiously looking at your experiences from an adult perspective and contemplating their healthiness instead of assuming normalcy. The insight derived from acknowledging these truths makes way for improved thinking and solving problems through a shift in your energy. This, in turn, places your goals nearer your reach while generating inner peace.

Trail Notes

- U How we view the world begins at birth and influences our beliefs and behaviors

- U Sometimes what we think is *normal* and *okay* isn't *healthy*

- U Childhood is similar to a puzzle where each piece is made up of a need or information

- U Our inner power comes from knowing why we do what we do

- U Sometimes what we most need to see is, at first, invisible

Chapter Two

By the Time I Get to My Emotions

Roadblocks to the Past

First grade arrived with the adventure of walking to school past the *witch's* house, a grassy tennis court, and two long fields over which I envisioned galloping a horse before arriving at our old brick schoolhouse called Benson, "Built in 1926" plastered on its front. Air raids prompted us to *duck and cover* under our desks and fire drills forced an enduring trapeze walk across a long, narrow bridge to safety. Benson was structurally condemned my fourth-grade year, creating the need for me to transfer to another school, though two more significant events occurred first: meeting my best friend, Dana, and publicly acting out for the first time.

Had my first-grade schoolteacher described me, shy, studious, petite, and likeable might have topped her list. Although I lost the election for class president because boys outnumbered girls, if you know what I mean, I didn't let that bother me. I excelled at other things, such as track and playing the Statue of Liberty at parent night, an honor made complete by the papier-mâché crown I made. On top of that, Ricky, the cutest boy in the class, liked me! I loved first grade. I finally felt as though I belonged somewhere. For a few hours each day, my anxiety and fear gave way to an innocence that allowed me to take pleasure in my world instead of worry about why my father and mother didn't get along.

The author, first grade

In second grade, the safety I felt at school permitted my pent up anger to break free. The unfortunate recipient was my classmate, Travis, who I pushed to the ground, sat on, and yanked out a wad of his hair. For weeks he walked around school with a bald spot on his head. I imagine the embarrassment of the smallest girl in class getting the better of him took a while to live down. No one seemed to realize the amount of self-control it took for me to hold in the depth of emotion I felt on a daily basis. I credit meeting my new friend Dana not long after that for the lack of another such incident. Dana taunted fate with a different type of trouble: Fizzies®, a tongue-staining candy-like disc that provided a context for limitless giggles and somewhat uninhibited participation in class. A much-needed distraction from my troubles, her outgoing personality gave me a fresh view of the world.

Before long, Dana and I acquired the nickname *the odd couple* due to her being the tallest girl in our class and my being the shortest. Almost overnight she became my pillar of strength and her home opted as my refuge. Our Saturday morning routine included walking around the downtown shops, then stopping to buy animal cookies and grapefruit soda on our way to her home where we set out our sleeping bags in the library of what seemed both an eerie and beautiful mansion. So prominent a three-story structure, I could see it all the way across town from my backyard, the location from which I would later watch it burn down, killing her grandmother. The top floor was a studio where her mother gave dance lessons and where a harboring bat once bit her father, an incident requiring numerous shots in his abdomen. The few times Dana and I snuck up there were short-lived due to imagining bats hanging from the ceiling, causing us to run back down the stairs, screaming all the way. Instinctively the follower in our duo, I allowed Dana's confidence to feed my idolization of her. Before long, she was telling me of someone she knew who owned a herd of wild horses and that, when I was ready, I could choose one for my own. After that, daydreams of packing my belongings, hitchhiking to the pasture, and jumping on my horse to gallop into happiness consumed much of my attention.

In time, the closing of Benson and Dana's desire to have more than one *best* friend threatened our relationship, generating my first taste of jealousy. With feelings of abandonment, hurt and self-doubt triggered by her absence, I began fifth grade at my new school hiding my emotion yet drowning inside from the anguish of feeling so alone in the changes occurring in my life. Helping to offset some of my pain was the luck of landing in a class-

The author and Dana, sixth grade

room with a cute, young male teacher fresh out of college. Perhaps due to my quiet demeanor, Mr. B seemed to pay more attention to me than he did others in the class, and certainly more than I was used to receiving. Being the first male adult I had been around other than my father and grandfather, I felt nervous in his presence and, even when enjoying the positive male influence I longed for, caution prevailed. While other girls in my class audaciously flirted with Mr. B with common schoolgirl crushes, I looked at him in a different light: as the father I craved.

By the following year, Mr. B's support had built up my confidence enough that I tried out for the cheerleading squad. Around the same time, however, I also found myself honored into a gang of girls known for the pranks they played. Our teacher, Ms. Elephant, as we re-named her, was our main target, though I'm not sure she deserved the amount of creativity we sent her way. Shooting spit wads in an attempt to hit her derriere and calling her different animal names depending on which wig she wore were just two of the acts in which I participated. I never dwelled on why. Even when my deeds landed me in the principal's office and my mother showed up, I simply told them I would stop, though I don't think I did. Having heard of my uncharacteristic behavior, Mr. B came to talk to me, his words still fresh in my mind today. "I hear you're being a pill." Though ashamed for disappointing him, a deeper feeling of anger dominated my logic, causing me to want to push him away, "What do you care?" But I didn't. Instead, I surrendered in an attempt to prove my worthiness to him, a need that penetrated my entire being.

I considered my best hope to be track season. *If only he saw how good I was,* I rationalized. *Maybe he would remain in my life.* Track was *my* sport. Unbeatable at Benson, I assumed this would continue at city trials. So when I placed only fourth in the 100-yard dash, I felt crushed. *Why can't I just be good at something*! I wanted to scream.

But, of course, I didn't. My voice was soft and flat and seldom did I speak unless spoken to first. And although probably meaning to inspire me, Mr. B's "you're going to have to do better than that" left me feeling defeated and powerless, causing me to see only one option: quitting track.

Soon thereafter, the first thought of suicide entered my mind. Friday nights in our town meant gathering at the sole high school to watch basketball. As I searched the stands to find a seat, my eyes stumbled upon Mr. B and his wife playing with their young child, an image of the perfect family. Overcome by my now familiar feelings of rage and envy, I paused at the stairwell, leaned over to view the three-story drop and, for a split second, contemplated jumping. In the realm of stopping my pain, I added death to my repertoire of options, right alongside riding a horse into the sunset.

When asked the benefit of examining one's childhood, I reply without hesitation, "No amount of money can buy you the degree of power over your life that you acquire when you know who you are." The next question usually goes something like this: "Well, if that's true, why don't more people look to the past for understanding?" And that's a question worth answering.

Not long ago my curiosity about that topic prompted me to send out a survey, albeit not a scientific one. I simply asked a variety of people via email the following question: "If you knew your life would benefit, what would stop you from exploring your childhood?" But before I tell you the results, please take a moment and answer that question for yourself.

🥾. *Exercise 2a: "If you knew your life would benefit, what would stop you from exploring your childhood?" Write your answer on your timeline.*

The results from my survey revealed one core reason for individuals not wanting to look back at their childhoods: emotions. Incidentally, this result did not surprise me. Emotions are common obstacles in my line of work. "Can't I just take a pill?" my patients often plead. And that always reminds me of the movie *Men in Black* with hunk Will Smith. I remember telling my therapist after watching the movie that he needed one of those magic wands so he could erase my past. How cool would that be, I thought. It would solve everything. I wouldn't have to feel any emotion because I wouldn't have any memories. At this point, Freud would probably comment how well I portrayed his theory of how people move *toward pleasure* and *away from pain*. That makes sense, right? Who wants to feel pain if they have a choice? This is *normal*. But the more important question becomes, is it healthy? Not always. Sometimes we have to move *through* pain to *get* to pleasure. A common example of this is grief, a topic we will discuss more in chapter ten. Grief requires a person to feel a series of emotions before having the ability to move forward less encumbered in life. Other difficult situations are similar. Any attempt to avoid, obscure, cover up, ignore, downplay, discount, overlook, disregard, shun, elude, circumvent, dodge, sidestep, or snub emotions usually has unfavorable consequences. The reason for this is simple: emotions serve vital functions.

For the next few minutes, consider what happens when you feel a strong emotion. Whether anger or joy, imagine energy in your body intensifying and surfacing to your awareness. Now, similar to a wild horse in a rodeo chute, this energy looks for an escape. You have a choice. Do you hold the emotion in or do you let it out? Either way, there are consequences. To avoid the impact of an emotion is virtually impossible – even if you do nothing.

One of the roles of emotions is *to help maintain mental strength and balance*. Think back to the emotion in your body. If you experience the emotion healthily, then the built-up energy naturally dissipates and your body returns to what I call *at peace,* or balanced. When you fail to experience the emotion healthily, the excess energy doesn't have anywhere to go, making it accumulate somewhere in your body. In time, this stress creates unhealthy consequences such as amplifying the original emotion (anger to rage) and/or displaying itself in physical form such as high blood pressure, insomnia, anxiety, and depression, to name a few. The elements to processing emotions healthily are:

1) feeling them,
2) understanding them, and
3) responding to them with *integrity*.

Let's say you feel angry and choose to respond by hitting someone. Your action most likely lacks integrity because, for one, it's illegal to assault someone. You might feel an emotional release, but you're most likely going to have to face other problems because of your action. Plus, hitting doesn't necessarily mean you understand your anger or that the reason for your anger is gone. On the other hand, if you feel angry, discover its origin, and resolve the issue in a healthy manner, your body then has the ability to return to its pre-anger state. The more unresolved emotions lurking in your body, the less peace you are apt to feel. And this brings us to the second yet no less important role of emotions: *to relay important information*.

The energy that rises to the surface of our awareness is sending us a message. Joy, for example, relays a positive occurrence. Common responses to joy are smiling, hugging, laughter, jumping up and down, or uninhibited *yippees*. There may be times when we need to restrain our demonstration of positive emotions, such as the time I was nine and laughed so hard I spit my milk out all over the lunchroom at school, but usually this upbeat energy is not problematic.

Negative energy, on the other hand, can be more troublesome. This is because we often allow the emotion to sway our actions. As in the previous example, just because we desire to hit someone when we feel angry doesn't mean hitting is a healthy response. What is important to remember is that our emotions don't tell us what to *do*; our emotions simply tell us how we *feel*. Have you ever heard the old adage *don't shoot the messenger?* Understanding the reasons behind our emotions allows us the opportunity to respond to them in non-offensive ways. Some people even use their negative energy to fuel positive endeavors. Candice Lightner used her anger and grief to do just that when she founded Mothers Against Drunk Drivers (MADD) after her daughter was killed by a drunk driver.

So, why don't more people respond healthily to their emotions? One reason is due to the judgment we place on them. Even the word *emotion* tends to have a negative connotation. Many of the responses to my survey referred to *the emotion it would bring up*. I don't know about you, but I'm not really thinking the responders were concerned with emotions such as happiness and joy. My guess is they were referring to perceived negative emotions such as anger, sadness, resentment, hate, shame, and envy, to name a few from the unpopular list. And I think the reason why people view emotions that way is because we do a pretty good job in our society at punishing, dismissing, modeling, and teaching the avoidance of such feelings. Thus, we don't learn how to respond to them in effective ways. What's the number one response when someone cries? "Oh, don't cry." Even when said with compassion, the ultimate message remains loud and clear: we prefer happy.

Before we continue with emotions, let's talk about some factors that influence us. Just as parents are powerful figures within a family, so too are societal beliefs significant in our lives. Rarely do we question the customs, traditions, and cultural norms that enmesh our lives. However, we're going to do just that. I believe that if something might stop me from benefiting my life, I want to understand why. First, though, we need more information, a situation that reminds me of something my grandfather said. "Knowledge is one of the only things you can carry with you that never becomes a burden." So far he has been right.

History shows we have endured some unhealthy social influences. Smoking was once so fashionable that a tobacco company named their cigarettes *Kool*. In time, the un-cool aspect of lighting up changed society's viewpoint. Today, smoke-free environments are our cultural norm. Now we are battling another unhealthy norm: obesity, stemming from our *clean your plate* mentality, love affair with fast food, sedentary life styles, and processed foods. Consequently, our government is now trying to change a strong and determined habit that affects nearly the entire population by increased health problems, lower productivity at work, increased insurance rates, and decreased pleasure. My point: just because something is widely accepted does not mean it is working in the best interest of individuals or society. Our ability to think critically, understand our behaviors and beliefs, and separate healthy from unhealthy allows us to make better choices for both ourselves and the *greater good*, a term I use for looking at how our decisions impact those around us as well as future generations. Now, back to emotions.

The idea of being able to look at emotions as necessary rather than annoyances was a huge wake-up call for me. Sitting in my therapist's office one day, he posed a question that initiated a lump in my throat, followed by my attempt to swallow it back down, a response to which I was proficient. "Just breathe," he assured me. Obediently following his instructions, breathing prevented me from being able to squash the emotion, and tears, much to my disgust, filled my eyes. As I instinctively attempted to wipe them away, he caught my hand in mid-air, "No. Let your tears fall. Feel your body cleansing the pain." And what occurred next was one of the few times to that point in my life I remember crying in front of someone. Mostly embarrassed, though partly relieved, I began looking at my tears differently. His statement gave me permission to feel what I was experiencing inside without negative judgment, and his words remain with me to this day. In fact, I often use similar words with my own patients: "Think of your tears as the sadness and unhappiness flowing out of your body."

Even though I first dreaded experiencing my tears, the more I cried, the easier it became because I began to feel the benefit. Familiarity allowed me to realize there was a reason for my tears. Prior to this, I believed that if I started crying I would never be able to stop or the effort would end up a painful and embarrassing waste of time. I had come to a place in my life where I felt my emotions were the only thing I had power over and that I was maintaining my sanity by holding onto them. The paradox of this belief was that by not allowing my tears to cleanse my body to make it stronger, I was actually making myself weaker. My symptoms of depression, anxiety, hopelessness, self-loathing, fear, worthlessness, and suicidal ideation were all consequences of my not allowing my body to naturally do what it was meant to do in order to maintain an emotional balance. My physical health, as well, endured negative consequences through weight loss, anxiety attacks, insomnia, restless leg syndrome, back and neck pain. I eventually learned that maintaining optimum mental health depends upon the continued interpretation of one's emotions.

> *Exercise 2b: Think of as many emotions as you can and write them on your timeline. Then, next to each emotion, write down a short statement defining how you generally respond to that emotion. For example, next to "joy", I would write "smile".*

CHAPTER TWO

While discovering my emotions, I not only realized I had learned to deny my sadness and anger, but in order to avoid bringing any attention to myself I also avoided joy, happiness, and other positive feelings. While I was growing up, people often commented on both my monotone voice and facial blankness. These attributes served me well as a child in remaining inconspicuous, a goal I equated to safety. As an adult, however, my expressionless demeanor has not been quite so advantageous unless playing poker.

When Gabe, my oldest son, became vertical around the age of one, he bestowed upon his father and me a new term. *Guk*, he showed us, was any unwanted item on the ground most likely destined for the vacuum cleaner. Whether motivated by boredom or the opinion his parents were untidy, Gabe walked around the house and picked up any piece of dirt, crumb, or paper off the carpet and brought it to one of us, placing it in our hands with a pronounced and educational, "*guk*." Years later in therapy, attempting to convey an unnamed feeling, I stumbled to find the right words. "Inside me is all this… this…" and the word "*guk*" blurted out, referring to all my unresolved issues, feelings, and emotions all rolled up into one. I envisioned this determined little tow-headed boy picking up all the garbage around the house and this visual gave me the strength to realize that I needed to acknowledge and discard all the *guk* lurking inside me. As if a dirty home, I needed to rid my body of that which was keeping me a less-healthy person and, more importantly, a less-present parent.

The consequences of avoiding our emotions are many. Without the intended relief our bodies gain when we healthily process emotions, *guk* collects inside us like gum under a school desk. This results in the pain Freud talked about which, in turn, lures us toward alternative self-soothing activities such as alcohol, drugs, food, sex, gambling, and over-spending, any of which can become problematic under the right circumstances. Incidentally, these behaviors are also known as *adult*

Gabe the "guk" guy at one year old

acting out. This failure to face our emotions — our humanness — robs us of our authenticity one feeling at a time. Our lives then become more complex and more problematical to control. Because emotions are what work to regulate the equilibrium of our true selves, these emotions are also what allow us to connect to ourselves. This means until we are able to do that, we will have more difficulty relating to others. Granted, facing your emotions might mean defying society's opinion about what is right and wrong, but wasn't smoking also *cool* once?

One of my more memorable patients was a woman who survived what I cannot describe as anything less than childhood torture. After a few sessions in which she sat silent and I talked, she returned for her next appointment, looked at me and boasted, "Do you want to know what's in my *guk* bag?" And the phrase stuck. *Guk* bag – that which holds the obstacles to one's authenticity.

Consider this: If you have issues in your life that won't go away, if you don't feel proud of whom you are, if you act impulsively rather than from a place of clear thought, or if you are aware of experiences that make you feel incomplete, you probably have some emotions to face. Emotions can serve as either roadblocks that defy your success or natural allies that dissolve the obstacles on your trail ride to personal freedom. The choice is yours.

Trail Notes

- Emotions maintain our body's stability and strength and relay important information

- Sometimes we have to move through pain to get to pleasure

- Knowledge is power

- Your actions affect you as well as the greater good

- *Guk* – unresolved issues, feelings, and emotions; *Guk* bag – that which holds the obstacles to your authenticity

Chapter Three
Ticket to Change
Tools to Grow By

Somewhere along the way, our family settled into a routine favoring silence and separateness. If not at home for a few days, I assumed my father was in the hospital again. I heard comments regarding *on* and *off* the wagon, but my mind visualized only a horse-drawn buckboard similar to the one Hoss drove into town on the television western, *Bonanza*. My father's employment status fluctuated as well. Comparable to most information that occurred in our family, his losing a prestigious accounting job with the county slipped out accidentally. Excitement over getting a new television set after thinking we had sold ours to someone who came and took it away turned out to be the repossession man confiscating items my father bought with money we didn't have. When attempting to sleep at night, my mother's pleas for my father to *change* spilled through the walls, though the context of the conversation was unclear. Most obvious was its one-sidedness and my mother's escalation in voice tone followed by tears as her words met prolonged quiet. Only once in my childhood did I witness any demonstrated affection between my father and mother. More common was a stagnant gloom that infiltrated our home like the haze left from my father's chain-smoking. Nurturing more secrecy were my grandfather's visits after church each Sunday. Somehow we all knew to disappear so he could impart what I suspect was spiritual guidance and wisdom to my father. It would be years before I learned it was my grandparents who were giving my father money to support our family, though I imagine he used it to adequately feed his cravings as well. *Enabling* was yet to be a fashionable term in the realm of addiction.

Due to our family's financial downfall, my mother spent most of the week commuting to a college seventy miles away in order to earn her teaching degree. Between traveling and studying, the role of my primary caregiver defaulted to my father, a position in which he had little interest. Asking him for lunch money he didn't want to part with and reminding him to pick me up after school proved pointless, prompting me instead to take coins off his dresser and walk the two miles home in the dark and often rain when he didn't show up. When I arrived home, he seldom uttered a word. I never knew if he realized he forgot to pick me up or if he just didn't care to acknowledge his error. Some days I found him passed out short of the front door, including one time when I discovered him still in the car with the motor on and the driver's side door wide-open. The only reason I knew he was alive was from the stench of stale alcohol that periodically escaped his mouth. After nudging his body for what seemed hours, he silently got out and stumbled inside.

As if a monumental event in history by which we mark time, I picture the true demise of our family the day the music died. Despite our vast dysfunction, the one constant in our household for years was my father's piano playing prior to dinner. As if giving a concert, he sat down on the piano bench, straightened his posture, and with poise, placed his hands over the keys. His music then mesmerized my body to a state of calm.

Captivated by how his fingers danced over the ivory, his talent humbled me equal to the embarrassment I felt at my lack of skill. At each of my piano recitals I wanted to shrink in humiliation as I imagined the audience whispering, "Oh, I would've expected better from the music teacher's granddaughter." It was true I thoroughly hated to play the piano in front of people. However, I loved to pretend to be brilliant like my father. Once, when I was about ten, I attempted to imitate his *Polonaise* by Chopin, playing the piece probably twenty times in a row, no doubt annoying everyone at home. Sometimes I wondered why my father didn't pursue music as a career, as it seemed to be the only time he did anything with passion. In stark contrast, reconciling this piano-playing man with the other father images I knew baffled me. Even though I imagine his early performances were indicative of his soberness, I don't believe I could otherwise tell a difference, for as soon as the concert was over, he returned to the distant sad man I never knew.

Over the years, my father's attempts at playing the piano grew into frustration as his fingers fell victim to his drinking. What began as a concert mood slowly descended into fear and apathy as his hands trembled and struck notes in error. Although I don't remember the exact day the music died, I know the tranquility that I once relished never returned.

If my father's music once brought our family solace, the dinner hour accentuated our misery. In her *everything is fine* pretense, my mother committed us to all sit down at the dinner table when she was home to replicate the perfect all-American family. This forced event molded the essence of our existence into my mind similar to a Norman Rockwell still photo, a likeness of which I once depicted in therapy:

Sitting in the corner with his back, ironically, to our church that resided across the street, my father's vacant expression resembled that of a curbside homeless man, powerless to his environment. Thin and malnourished, he picked at his food as might a three year old who didn't like the menu, though my mother's glare made it clear that the discomfort he would feel if he left the table would be far worse than riding out the dinner hour. Noticeably in some stage of intoxication, his attempts at holding his head up by bracing his arm against the wall often failed, resulting in a *thud* sound that everyone disregarded along with his coughing, moaning, and nausea. My oldest sister sat next to my father and probably displayed the most honest communication at the table. Her gestures materialized in the form of facial expressions or comments insinuating she'd rather be anywhere else. Obviously challenging authority yet careful not to ignite battle, she would eventually retreat to complacency. My other sister sat across from my father and was, according to studies on group dynamics, the one called *the peacemaker*. Her gift was attempting to make everyone feel special all the while ignoring the tension that she felt so committed to deflate. For unknown reasons, perhaps being born last or maybe just the most convenient place for a highchair, I sat at the head of the table facing everyone else. Uncomfortable in that it was the only escape route for my father and oldest sister, I kept one leg on the side of my chair, readying myself to spring to my feet in case my mother's covert mission exploded. Meanwhile, my mother bustled around the kitchen similar to a border collie attempting to keep her sheep from straying, seldom joining us for more than a few minutes at a time. Eventually our dinner ritual yielded to 'busy schedules and teenage rebellion', though I now suspect these were simply justifications for my mother's waning energy.

Pretend you are beginning a new adventure. Can't think of one? Okay, I'll choose one for you. Surprise! You're going to buy a horse. So, where to start? There is preparation if you want the best outcome. As with most new endeavors, the more knowledge you have, the better.

What breeds of horses are there? How much do they cost? What type of riding interests you? What do horses eat? What kind of equipment do you use? What kind of care do they need? These questions skim the surface of what horse owners need to be aware of before purchasing a horse. Failure to understand the needs of a horse can be dangerous for the rider, expensive for the owner, and costly for the horse. Boy Scouts had something going in their favor when they adopted the motto, *Be Prepared*. Looking back at one's childhood is no different. Fortunately, unlike buying a horse, there is no expense. All it takes is effort.

If you missed it before, I'll say it again: *Knowledge is underrated*. Desperately wanting a horse, I bought my first steed without riding him first. Perhaps his name should have been a clue: Thunder. But young and foolish and consumed by my life-long dream, I simply saw a beautiful black quarter horse in the pasture for sale and, as they say, *the rest is history*. Besides loving them, however, I knew little about horses. When I rode Thunder for the first time, all was fine as he began walking down this trail with me wobbling on his back until suddenly he did an about-turn and began galloping the other way. When pulling the reins and yelling *whoa* failed to muster a response from him, I held on tightly and hoped he tired easily. Beginner's luck, I imagine, kept me from kissing dirt. Once stopped, it seemed as though he looked at me to say, "Okay, what do you want me to do next?" Little did I know I had inadvertently given him a barrel-racing cue with my legs. Looking back, I realize how lucky I was not to have been injured or killed. I also realize that Thunder paid a price for my ignorance. Thirty years and numerous horses later, I acknowledge I could've been a better owner had I a greater knowledge base. I was what is often considered a negative term: *ignorant*. In truth, *ignorance* simply means *a lack of knowledge*. And, as I may have hinted at before, the power of knowledge is immeasurable. Consider this: if we base our actions on what we know, then the more we know, the better-informed decisions we can make. Just as with buying a horse, there are certain topics of value that precede success when exploring your childhood. One of these topics is *parenting* because parents, a term I use to include all caregivers, have the most influence over us as we grow up. So, here goes…

There are no perfect parents. There, I said it. And I hope not too many of you are offended. It's just that parenting is, well, impossible to do perfectly.

The author riding Thunder

There are too many variables, too much to know, and never enough time. Let's face it, children are needy little creatures. Not only that, but their needs change. It's similar to learning to play a new game and then, just when you're catching on, someone changes the rules. Then again, I've met some wonderful parents who, humbly, are the first to suggest they don't know it all. Their most endearing qualities are these: a desire to know more, be accountable, and learn from their mistakes. In fact, that isn't such a bad philosophy for life. It reminds me of one of my favorite sayings: *Perfection is an aspiration, not a destination.*

I once heard parenting called *the most difficult job one will ever be honored to have*. I agree with that statement. But before I continue with my beliefs on parenting, let's find out what you think.

👢 *Exercise 3a: If you wrote a job description for parents, what would it say? Add this to your timeline.*

Whether you are a parent or just experienced parents, everyone has expectations about what a parent *should* be. This is an important question because, as mentioned earlier, it is our beliefs that influence our behaviors. One of my beliefs about parenting, for example, is that feeding a child is a parent's job. You may be thinking, "Duh….," but I assure you, I have worked with parents who, unfortunately, failed to take this responsibility seriously.

🥾 *Exercise 3b: As you consider your beliefs about parenting, think about where your beliefs originated. Do they stem from your parents? A friend? An expert? Something you read? Add your answers to your timeline.*

Be assured, there are no right or wrong answers. What you are finding is your *baseline*. Some people might not really know their beliefs. That's okay. Others might acknowledge their thoughts about parenting but aren't sure where they came from or if they agree with them because they've never thought about them before. That's okay too. The objective is for you to understand your current beliefs about parenting, nothing more. It's similar to someone asking me my opinion about monster truck engines. *They're big?* Honestly, my beliefs are minimal because it's not a topic I analyze. But ask me what I think about horse racing and you'd better sit down and get comfortable.

I sum up my current baseline regarding parenting this way: I believe parenting is a choice that requires a committed selflessness to make one's child a priority, understanding that every decision made as a parent has either a direct or indirect affect on the child. Furthermore, I believe the goal of parenting is to prepare one's child to become an independent, emotionally healthy, socially conscious, responsible, productive adult. My short version, however, is this: *to nurture, educate, and support a child toward authenticity.*

My baseline today regarding parenting is actually quite different from what my baseline was when I had my children. In fact, I don't remember thinking about what parenting meant when I became a mother. Like most new parents, the basis for what I knew came from my own upbringing – on what was *normal* from my childhood. Luckily, my friend Tess was there to teach me healthier and more effective child rearing practices. Realizing my ignorance, I began studying as much as I could about children in an attempt to enhance my skills.

Knowing your baseline gives you a point from which to begin. By asking yourself *what* you believe, you are then challenged to ask yourself *why* you believe that something. This, in turn, gives you additional insight into your past. Ultimately, understanding your *whats* and *whys* regarding parenting will help you differentiate between *normal* and *healthy*, an important aspect in the process of self-discovery. Imagine, for example, you believe it is okay for parents to tell their children they are *stupid*. When considering *why* you believe this, you realize it's because your parents called you *stupid,* thus, it seems *normal*. The goal is then to question the healthiness of such a statement. You'll find the next few chapters designed with this task in mind. Questioning your beliefs lets you think about your childhood objectively, ultimately allowing you to discover what's in your *guk* bag. When I realized that most people didn't share my level of anxiety while riding in a car, for example, I felt compelled to find out why I was different. This led me to understand how my anxiety began as well as pointed me to other areas of concerning behavior in the process. Positive outcomes such as this one also allowed me to think of *ignorance* in a new light. Now when I don't know something, I'm not shy about asking myself the *what* and *why* questions. I feel empowered when I know why I believe what I do. Plus, when I'm not sure of my beliefs, I'm plagued by a little voice that says: *If you don't know what you believe in, you might fall for anything.*

Perhaps by now you can understand my passion for knowledge and appreciate its value. In today's world of the internet and being able to type in one word and receive twenty-three gazillion references regarding any given topic, a lack of information is inexcusable. This doesn't mean you are expected to be an expert on everything, of course. It simply means the availability of information is at one's fingertips – literally. This amazes me because I remember spending many of my college days at the library looking through card catalogs and microfiche, then waiting days or weeks for the articles to arrive. Okay, I also remember typewriters and how excited I was when I bought one that automatically erased twenty-five characters with the push of a key. *That* was awesome. My point is, sometimes the only thing holding us captive from reaching our dreams is knowledge. However, if knowledge is readily available, then the only thing *really* holding us back is ourselves. If this is the situation in your life, the question of *why* is worth asking. *Why* am I not seeking the answers I need for an improved life? This answer to *why* often allows for an important piece of your puzzle to be unveiled: *awareness*. Without awareness, the opportunity to problem solve does not exist. I could not resolve my anxiety while riding in a car, for example, until I realized it was problematic.

To help boost your awareness, you will need two tools. And no, you don't need to go to a hardware store. You actually already possess these tools and carry them with you wherever you go. They reside in your most coveted asset: your brain. They are *analyzing* and *objectivity*. While some people commonly use these skills in everyday life, we don't always think about the fact we are using them, nor do we define exactly what we are doing when we do use them. For clarity, then, I'm going to do just that:

Analyzing: *to examine something in detail in order to understand it better.*

Objectivity: *the ability to perceive something without being influenced by personal emotions or prejudice.*

As with most tools, we gain precision by practicing. Are you ready?

🐾 *Exercise 3c: You will use this exercise throughout your trail ride to discover your childhood story. I call it "Processing a Story" (PAS) and there are five easy steps:*

1) Choose an experience from your childhood and think about everything that occurred.

2) Limit everything you thought about to only facts. (I find this exercise easiest if I pretend I'm reading a screenplay. In looking at the scenario where the police arrested my father, for example, it might sound like this: A father is driving down the road intoxicated with a gun in the car when a lit-up police car approaches. The father pulls off the road and stops. A young child crawls into the back seat and hides.) You are simply telling the story without judgment or emotion.

3) Now consider the healthiness of your experience. (In my story, for example, one of the areas of concern is the fact that a young child is riding in a car with an intoxicated person. Another area of concern would be the gun in the car.)

4) Visualize the scenario again, this time paying attention to your body's reaction and what you felt. Try to remember both your positive and negative feelings at the time of the experience. For me, it helps to close my eyes and visualize the event when I do this.

5) Lastly, consider the impact of this experience on you. Did your worldview change? Did any of your beliefs or behaviors change? Was any emotion left unresolved? What was the outcome of the experience?

The ultimate goal of PAS (processing a story) is this: to identify unwanted emotion, faulty beliefs, and unwelcome behaviors that originated from unhealthy childhood events. These are what make up the missing, damaged, or misplaced puzzle pieces in your *guk* bag. An important factor when processing your childhood stories is to not place any time limit. It takes as long as it takes to get to the bottom of the *whats* and *whys* of your childhood experiences. Easy, huh? And remember, try not to underestimate the value of any experience you analyze. Self-exploration is most beneficial when you analyze what you perceive to be both *healthy* and *unhealthy* experiences.

Recently becoming an avid football fan, I look at this process similar to that of the replay referee in the NFL who has the ability to analyze a play from every angle in order to come to an unbiased conclusion. The referee may personally prefer one team to the other, but the game's accurate outcome relies on the referee's ability to be objective. This is your job as well in looking back at your childhood. The value of exploring events without labeling them as good, bad, right, or wrong is crucial because when we jump to conclusions we tend to end the flow of any additional information that comes our way. The minute your mind tells you, *she's wrong* or *it's his fault* and you accept it, your focus changes from information gathering to judgment. This is not the intent of looking back at your childhood at this point. There will come a time where we need to approach the topic of blame, but right now your job is to become *the greatest information gatherer that ever lived* because you first need to understand the truth. When I am tempted to place blame, I try to remember these words: *Inquire, don't judge.* There is no doubt in my mind that inquiring about why, who, where, what, and when will be more helpful to you in almost any facet of life than placing blame, especially initially.

Exercise 3d: In exercise 1c, I asked you to think about six characteristics that describe who you are. Now ask two friends you trust to do the same in regards to you, three positive characteristics and three characteristics they view would benefit from improvement. Sometimes it is difficult for us to see certain aspects of ourselves. The more honest your friends are, the more helpful the information will be for you. Write their responses next to yours on your timeline. As you compare your self-assessed characteristics to those your friends gave you, consider the similarities and differences. If you aren't clear about or disagree with a characteristic given to you by one of your friends, ask for examples. Try to see yourself through their eyes. Becoming aware of how other people view us is of great value in being better able to understand ourselves.

One important thought: this is a personal journey. I won't say *not* to share your findings with others, but I caution you about allowing other people to input their judgment. The experiences you are looking at need to be about what *you* see, *you* think, *you* believe, and *you* feel, not someone else's opinions. If you desire support or need someone to go along on your trail ride, I recommend you find a mental health professional.

Being mindful of wanting to hurry is also significant. Self-discovery is a process. An ongoing joke in our family developed when I began overseeing my sons' writing assignments for school. Apparently, common thought among teenagers is that one can write a prolific essay in thirty minutes. In an attempt to dislodge this defective train of thought, I spent many hours teaching them the benefit of getting words down on paper, editing, the concept of a rough draft, more editing, the final draft, proofreading, editing, and finally, the finished essay ready to turn in. "Writing," I insisted, "is a process." And, of course, they made fun of me. Upon seeing their returned assignments with high marks, however, they began to see the value of my obsession. Today, both are accomplished writers, though even while in their MBA programs they never missed a chance to tease me about the *process* when writing a paper. So, the moral of this story is: even if, like my sons, you don't share my enthusiasm about processes, try to take a deep breath and just go with it. Some of life's greatest endeavors have resulted from processes. Do you think Edison sat down one day and simply invented the phonograph? Nope. From his New Jersey laboratory, Edison invented some memorable items that we still use today, such as the light bulb, the phonograph, and the movie camera. But he also made some less impressive inventions along the way, such as his biggest failures, the magnetic iron-ore separator and concrete furniture. But the point is he never gave up. The reason why people know who he is today is because he kept trying. His perseverance to continue from one idea to another led him to greatness. I imagine he became frustrated at times. Perhaps he even felt he would never succeed. And while not all of his inventions became popular, he patented a new invention every two weeks during his working career. Just imagine if he would have stopped at his first failure or never tried at all. I don't know about you, but I'm grateful he continued his processes in order to benefit the world. Self-discovery is similar. Self-discovery gives you the opportunity to improve your life one step at a time while generating widespread triumphs along the way.

So, do you remember that horse you were going to buy? Well, I'm pleased to announce that your steed is now in your backyard and that you have learned how to giddee-up. Unfortunately, you do not yet know how to steer efficiently. That's why in the next few chapters you will learn what to look for on your trail ride so you can maneuver smoothly through any obstacles you encounter. As with Edison, you will probably find some things that don't work well and have to adjust your problem solving approach. Using the tools you previously learned in this chapter will assist you in finding what works and what doesn't work. This process will then allow you to arrive at your desired destination: your true self. My suggestion? Hold on and enjoy the ride! I guarantee that the result will be worth your effort.

CHAPTER THREE

Trail Notes

- Ignorance simply means lacking knowledge

- Perfection is an aspiration, not a destination; inquire don't judge

- Tools for your ride: Awareness, Analyzing, Objectivity, and Processing a Story (PAS)

- A parent's job is to nurture, educate, and support a child to authenticity

- Discovering your true self is a process

Chapter Four

You Messed Up My Life

Healthy, Dysfunctional, and Abusive

If sixth grade bred mischievous acts, middle school brought about an unexpected surrender to conventionalism. With the *gang* having disbursed, my attention veered toward grades and peer pressure. Indicative of a pre-teenager trying to fit in, I assumed the role of my latest admiration and attempted to imitate make-up and fashion styles. Thankfully, few of my inventions made it out the front door. Stronger than my need for conformity was my desire to avoid unsolicited notice. Even a hair trim caused me anxiety due to the judgment I might receive. Social gatherings and sleepovers caused the most concern, however, due to my not feeling as though I could reciprocate invitations because of my father's unpredictable behavior. And, in time, my peers quit asking for my presence. Although Dana and I attended the same school again, and I met a lifelong friend in my new locker mate, Tess, my once-promising middle school adventure slowly disintegrated over three years into disappointment and despair.

While avoiding socialization became my norm, my sisters each responded to the tension in our home differently. Now driving, my oldest sister used her freedom to escape the confines of her discomfort and sometimes volunteered to take me with her. Even though our conversations skirted any topic that might dare penetrate the core of our misery, I grew to think of us as friends and savored the attention she gave me as we drove around the city with no apparent destination. Similar to each other in that we both craved a sense of belonging, our differing paths toward this elusive goal ultimately undermined our sisterhood in the years to come.

Three years older than me, my middle sister was the most outgoing of us siblings. With a close group of friends, she spent much of her time socializing and studying, easily landing the *most likely to succeed* crown in our family. When at home, I often found her reading fiction, perhaps her escape from reality, though I viewed her books as my rival, and my frustration grew when she chose them over me. Mainly, though, I envied her ability to empathize with what ailed our family. Whatever she did with the poison infiltrating our household, it seemed to work for her. She was the daughter people praised, the daughter people wanted to be around, and the one my grandmother pitted against me. Showing no apparent emotional wounds, one might have thought she grew up in a different home. Over time, despite my admiration of her, I also came to resent her natural resilience, and this tore at the strength of our relationship.

As seventh grade ended, Dana asked me to spend the summer with her at her aunt and uncle's home in San Diego. Not ever having left Oregon, the idea of going somewhere new tested my belief that *the grass must be greener somewhere else.* Instead, I found another safe venue for liberating my emotions, similar to the incident in second grade when I pulled Travis' hair out. This time I found myself sobbing uncontrollably in the bathroom of a movie theatre after watching *Love Story,* a reaction stemming from a place other than the doomed storyline. My feelings for Dana's uncle were equally concerning, bearing a similarity to how I viewed Mr. B back in fifth grade. Watching him brush his little girl's hair and read her stories caused the likes of poisonous venom to rip through my body, challenging me to scream, "Why do you get a father that takes care of you and I don't?" Fearful at some point my feelings might escape my control, I began scrutinizing my every move, as if an escaped convict attempting to avoid capture. By the end of summer, my once-hopeful escapade to San Diego served only to further my dislike for the person living inside me.

The author, eighth grade

Eighth grade began on the upbeat of my fluctuating moods. I am still unsure what possessed me to try out for the cheerleading squad, but I define the moment I heard my name called over the loudspeaker as one of the winners by popular vote as the most blatantly unexpected of my life. I couldn't reconcile why so many virtual strangers liked me when the message at home concluded I wasn't worthy of notice. I even considered the possibility that someone miscounted the votes.

Within seconds my life changed. Girls I barely knew wanted to be my friends, boys asked me to the movies, and I found myself in the spotlight for school activities. Watched and scrutinized, I eventually broke under the pressure. Feeling undeserving and fake, I wanted to explain: *I'm not who you think I am. I don't know how to live up to this person you like.* I felt as though I was attempting to live the dream of other girls who had mothers to teach them how to be confident and feminine, and fathers to protect them and support their dreams. What did I know about being social? Up until junior high, after all, my existence focused on strolling my neighborhood topless pretending to be an Indian from the 1800s in search of her horse. Despite feeling proud to be a part of something for the first time, my achievement also doubled as a defense against my family. *See, I'm not a loser. See, people actually like me. See, I must not be as ugly as you make me feel.* Eventually, however, my mother validated my fraud at one of our football games when she demeaned me for not looking professional as I ate popcorn between cheers. Humiliated, I rejected any desire to try harder.

Eighth grade also brought the start of my period. Not knowing why girls menstruated in the first place, and having developed a stubborn independence, I kept it a secret. I knew only that girls wore big pads in their panties attached to elasticized belts. Given that, I simply stuck one of the pads in my underwear without the belt and tried to walk in such a way it wouldn't slip, a feat that took some skill I might add. All was fine until science class when a boy I liked put his hand on my chair right before I sat down. Under normal circumstances, his prank may have amused me because he was cute. On this particular day, however, I was mortified when I was sure he felt the diaper-like garment underneath my skirt. Unable to face my shame, I never talked to him again. Months later, I heard some girls in the bathroom talking about tampons, or *plugs* as they so delicately called them, and after an embarrassing trip to the drugstore, I explicitly followed the directions and received an overdue anatomy lesson.

By the end of the school year, each morning forced a challenge to survive the day. My past thought of jumping down the stairwell had multiplied into numerous fantasies about death. Tired of not fitting in, I surrendered into a solitary world of my own, certain of eventual doom. After walking home from school in the dark, rain, and cold after my father failed to show up again I found a half-full bottle of pain relievers, swallowed them, and went to bed. No preceding thought entered my mind other than not wanting to feel any more pain. When I awoke miserably sick during the night, I realized my attempt to kill myself was yet another one of my failures, as well as an occurrence no one ever noticed.

Sharing was my favorite part of the day while serving as a mental health specialist for Head Start, the federally funded preschool program for children at risk. There is nothing quite like four and five year olds telling stories about their lives. They are direct, honest, and non-judgmental. "My dad robbed a store last night, then the police came and took him to jail." No hesitation or embarrassment; just excited to be center stage to share their *normalcy*. The first time I heard such a story, my heart sank. That's when I began questioning at what age children discover that *normal* may not always be *healthy*. What I found is, too often, they don't. Most of us, in fact, reach adulthood with some faulty perceptions about our childhoods. This is inevitable given the limitations of a child's brain and the power of parental and societal influences. Unless we identify these faulty perceptions in adulthood, they remain problematic, keeping us from making critical connections between our current problems and our childhood experiences.

Before we continue, I need to address a related topic that I briefly mentioned before. Discussing unhealthy aspects of your childhood may bring up the question of blame. Some people, in fact, believe blame is inevitable when looking back at one's childhood. After all, if some past experience results in a missing, damaged, or misplaced puzzle piece, there must be someone to blame, right? Well, yes, no, and maybe. If I sound vague, it's because every person's childhood story is unique. Only the truth can accurately guide you. This means blame is one possible aspect to your puzzle, though not a certainty. Having said that, blame is not a topic we can fully appreciate until we reach that point on our trail ride. For now, I would like to ask that you don't let the issue of blame be a roadblock for your learning and information gathering. When the time is appropriate, I will address blame in more detail and give it the attention it deserves.

Exercise 4a: Think of five goals that would improve your life and write them on your timeline. Next to each goal, write down any roadblock(s) that stand in your way of achieving that goal. In other words, why haven't you already accomplished these goals?

This exercise serves two important purposes. First, it helps you think about how you want to design your life, and second, it helps you think about what stands in your way. Keep in mind some of your missing, damaged, or misplaced puzzle pieces from your childhood might make up these roadblocks. When my anxiety about riding in a car became problematic, for example, I set a goal to find a way to feel more relaxed while a passenger. In other words, I wanted to reduce my racing heart and clenching of the seat cushion while envisioning the hundreds of ways we could crash. My roadblock was my ignorance. I didn't know how to decrease my intrusive level of anxiety. This made my *car anxiety* one of my damaged puzzle pieces. While some anxiety may be healthy while riding in a car, mine was overbearing. Eventually, with the help of a therapist, I lowered my anxiety to a tolerable level. I then considered this damaged puzzle piece to be *me healthy,* a term I use to signify an acceptable level of healthiness. While my anxiety when riding in a car may never fall to a tranquil level, the amount of anxiety I now experience is acceptable to me because I have power over it rather than it having power over me. Make sense? Similar to an injury that leaves a scar, some of your past *guk* may not disappear completely, but that doesn't mean you can't still be healthy, strong, and in control of your life.

Although the presence of unhealthiness in one's childhood is more common than not, you may have learned not to question what's behind you. I once heard a patient's friend scold her while in the waiting room, "Oh, grow up! When are you going to quit living in the past?" This comment actually amused me because I thought the patient *was* 'growing up' by attempting to understand how her childhood was holding her back in life. In my experience, people who criticize or demean others with *get over your childhood* type statements are usually avoiding a need to look at their own roadblocks. As nice as it would be if our childhood issues automatically self-corrected at the age of eighteen so we could all grow into healthy, happy, whole adults, I don't believe that pill yet exists. As far as I know, the only solution for *not* living in the past is resolving the issues from childhood that still negatively affect us today. Consider this: any reason for *not* looking back at your childhood may actually be a disguised piece of *guk* that is preventing you from enjoying a more successful future. In other words, sometimes you have to look back before you can move forward.

In order to understand your childhood, it is first important to become familiar with three terms we commonly hear to describe families: *healthy, dysfunctional,* and *abusive.* The following definitions are relative to parenting because parents are ultimately responsible for children. As you read them, remember that *ignorance* simply means *lacking knowledge.*

Healthy Family: *Developmentally appropriate parenting.*

Dysfunctional Family: *Developmentally inappropriate or ignorant parenting.*

Abusive Family: *Developmentally inappropriate or ignorant parenting that is a legal offense.*

Given these definitions, you may be wondering what is meant by the term *developmentally*. *Developmentally* speaks to a period of time within which a child has the ability to understand concepts necessary for healthy growth. In other words, leaving a two year old home alone is not a *developmentally* sound decision because a two year old does not have the ability to comprehend safety issues. On the other hand, leaving a child who is ten home alone *may* or *may not* be *developmentally* appropriate depending on the child's level of maturity and the length of time left unattended.

Along with *healthy, dysfunctional,* and *abusive*, another category worth mentioning is what I call *childhood intrusions*. This category includes incidents such as accidents, relocation, illness, parental marriage/divorce, house fires, acts of nature, war, job loss, death, and terrorism. Because of the increased stress these events usually cause, the way in which a parent responds to them can affect a child's development. This also makes them important events for using PAS (processing a story). *Childhood intrusions* are commonly memorable events as well and can aid you in constructing benchmarks on your timeline.

Exercise 4b: Think of any childhood intrusions you experienced growing up and add them to your timeline at the age they occurred.

CHAPTER FOUR

The goal of this chapter is to set forth the skill set for you to be able to tell the difference between *healthy* and *unhealthy*. This will allow you to examine your childhood and discover your truths. These truths, in turn, will unveil the missing, damaged, and misplaced puzzle pieces needing your attention. So, here goes. As I describe the following terms, consider your childhood experience.

Healthy families are able to talk about any topic, they are consistent, their verbal and nonverbal language complements the other, the parents model the behavior expected of the child, they are honest, they support and promote age-appropriate independence and education, they respect privacy and boundaries, they endorse freedom of expression, and they teach mutual respect.

Unhealthy family characteristics, in contrast, include anything that interferes with healthy family functioning such as ambiguous messages, parents who act one way but want their children to act another, secrets, children taking on non-child roles or not being able to speak their thoughts, submissive or overly-dominant parents who prevent age-appropriate independence and education, lack of privacy and boundaries, disrespect, and inappropriate punishment. While all of these characteristics are considered *dysfunctional,* some of them could also be labeled *abusive* depending on the circumstances. Sometimes only a fine line separates *dysfunction* from *abuse*.

Abuse includes a wide range of behaviors, from the father who humiliates his son by calling him *stupid* to the mother who drowns her children. A general working definition of abuse for our purposes is *the maltreatment of a minor for which there is legal recourse*. Forms of abuse include physical, sexual, psychological (emotional), neglect, and abandonment. Child abuse laws were established to protect children due to their vulnerability, and anyone who suspects abuse can make a report to police or an agency sanctioned to protect children.

🥾 *Exercise 4c: Given the definitions of healthy, dysfunctional, abusive, and childhood intrusions, how would you describe your childhood? This will be your baseline definition. I might have described my baseline as "healthy with some possible dysfunction" had I described it before therapy. The reason for this is that I did not yet understand the difference between normal and healthy. I, like many people, did not correlate the cause of my adult problems as having originated in childhood. I also did not realize the truths of my childhood yet, so many of my beliefs were faulty. Today I describe my childhood as "mostly dysfunctional with some abuse and a few intrusions" when I am asked.*

While I wrote this book for anyone regardless of particular childhood experiences, I believe it is important to acknowledge child abuse in our country because it founds the extreme need for some form of social change – a change that begins with you and me. On any given day in the United States, approximately five children die of abuse. In Arizona where I live, three children on average die each month. Recently, one little girl suffocated after being stuffed in a box because she took a Popsicle without permission, another child died after his head was slammed against a door by his father, and a young boy was drugged and left in the woods to die. Sadly, all states have similar tragic stories. My thought is this: if five children die each day in our country due to child abuse, imagine the number of children who *live* with abuse. Then consider the number of children who must live with some form of dysfunction. This heartbreaking reality validates why more adults don't naturally look to their childhoods for answers to their unhappiness. Many view their *unhealthy* experiences in childhood as *normal* and fail to realize the origin of their lost potential.

Unhealthiness can be subtle in its presence. If parents are imperfect and children model their behavior after them, it stands to reason that all childhoods produce beliefs and behaviors worthy of a better understanding. I had a patient once who told me she thought her childhood was wonderful. When she hit her twenties, however, she began having conflict with her parents after she changed her political affiliation. Her parents argued *they taught her better than that* and *how dare she disrespect her family*. What my patient eventually realized was that she had never outwardly disagreed with her parents before because she felt this was disobeying them. While growing up she kept her opinions to herself in order to avoid conflict. In time, her parents agreed to come to therapy and they acknowledged that they had not promoted their daughter's freedom of expression. I admire these parents for working toward a healthier relationship with their daughter. I like to remind parents that it is *okay* to admit imperfection. In fact, parents who admit their faults and then learn from them model an important lesson for children. This act of acknowledging humanness is a precursor to procuring both connectedness and healthy forgiveness, a topic covered in chapter thirteen.

Exercise 4d: Read the characteristics of healthy, dysfunctional, and abusive families again. Now, pretend you are a stranger walking into your house when you were a child. Choose a memorable day. Apply PAS (processing a story) from chapter three. What did you learn?

One of my favorite experts in the field of child abuse recovery is psychologist Alice Miller. Her book, *The Truth Will Set You Free*, opened my eyes to the importance of truth telling and her book's title easily became my motto. Freud said something similar: "Being entirely honest with oneself is a good exercise." The value in discovering your truth is that it helps unveil the *guk* in your life. This, in turn, gives you the opportunity to resolve the underlying unhealthiness and become closer to your authentic self. If you want to gain unparalleled power over your life, no other concept in this book is more important than *truth finding*.

The irony in truths and untruths is that they both contain immeasurable power. While truth strengthens one's sense of self, untruths in the form of lies, secrets, and silence promote self-destructiveness. Consider a time you either told a lie or kept a secret that resulted in guilt, shame, embarrassment, worry, nausea, headache, anxiety, or even anger. You may have even felt forced to lie again in order to cover up the first untruth. I know I have had such experiences. These acts have one common factor: the inner conflict they produce takes us farther away from our genuine selves. This is why uncovering the truth in your childhood benefits you. If the truth remains buried, whether through ignorance, denial, or choice, the consequences are bound to create a roadblock in your life.* Such was the case in chapter one when the woman's ignorance landed her in a domestic violence environment, ultimately causing her to lose her home and children. Had this woman understood the unhealthiness of her father's physical violence instead of believing it was normal, perhaps her story would've ended differently. Instead, her actions allowed the cycle of unhealthiness to continue.

Truth finding requires both self-honesty and the acceptance that other people may not agree with your truths. People who knew me as a child, for example, may remember some of the events I describe in this book differently. And that's fine. That is their perception. How many times have you watched a sporting event with someone and ended up disagreeing with each other on how a referee called a play? My truth is my perception of an occurrence. My perception of my childhood

---

*An exception to this is in the case of trauma where there are repressed memories. Such cases require a mental health professional for guidance. Sometimes repressed memories are best left repressed.

experiences is what founded my behaviors and beliefs. Whether I misinterpreted a situation or saw a reality that no one validated is relatively unimportant compared to understanding the meaning I placed on the experience. What is of value when looking at your past is to process your truth so that you can make sense out of your initial response to the situation as well as the consequences that materialized because of your response. This ultimately permits you to discern between the normalcy and the healthiness of these behaviors, allowing you a better understanding of yourself. My point? Sometimes truth finding is a lonely task because only you can identify your truth. In other words, finding someone to agree with your childhood experiences isn't part of this process. Your trail ride is a solo journey unless you request the guidance of a mental health professional.

Not long ago I had a conversation with a marketing consultant in the publishing world who eagerly told me everything I was doing wrong in preparing my book for publication. After a few minutes of his lecture, I realized a couple of my triggers were gearing up and I felt myself shrink to that of a child scolded by an authority figure. With my mind going numb to rebuttal, though knowing deep in my gut that I had a legitimate defense somewhere in my brain, I slowly shut down, succumbing to his bullying. After hanging up with him, I took refuge in an email to my mentor telling him of the incident and that I was now questioning my truth. He replied with two simple words: *stand tall*. And to this day these two words continue to inspire me to believe in myself. No one has the right to tell you *your* truth. You are the only one in the world who knows what you think and feel. To feel ashamed of where you've been, what you've experienced, or who you are decreases your ability to find inner peace.

Childhoods are rarely all good or all bad. Humanness is just not set up that way. We are fascinating, complex, imperfect, emotional beings. To question what is *healthy* and *unhealthy* is healthy. The odds your childhood holds valuable answers to your untapped potential are in your favor. For every person who grew up in an abusive environment, whose needs weren't met, or who felt obligated to keep family secrets, exploring your childhood truths is the beginning of a more gratifying future.

CHAPTER FOUR

Trail Notes

- ⋃ Missing, damaged, or misplaced puzzle pieces make up your roadblocks to happiness

- ⋃ All childhoods have unhealthy aspects; parents and society are powerful influences

- ⋃ Oftentimes you can't move forward in life until you look back

- ⋃ Understanding healthy from unhealthy is one of the keys to authenticity

- ⋃ The truth will set you free; stand tall

Chapter Five

Great Balls of Energy

Acting Out – Looking Inward

High school began with my stubborn resistance repelling conformity like bullets hitting an armored car. No longer did I listen to people who thought they knew what I needed. The cliques, games, and pretenses that motivated the behavior of my peers did not impress me, and the idea of participating in any school offerings seemed out of reach. I was the self-imposed bottom rung of the caste system, leaving the chance of my fitting in as dismal as my parents buying me a horse. Dances came and went void of my attendance, no boys asked me out, none of my family questioned my unpopularity, and I was simply relieved to maintain my anonymity. Enjoyment required an entity absent from my life for some time.

At the core of my torment was the reoccurring image of my father kicking our dog Mike out the back door after his aging hips kept him from moving quickly enough. The meek man who normally cowered to all confrontation had taken out his whiskey-driven supremacy on a defenseless dog, betraying his undying loyalty. Fearing what I was capable of, I restrained my raging anger and did nothing, leaving me to wonder if I was any different from this man I now detested. Shortly thereafter, one of my parents had Mike euthanized, and upon arriving home from school I was greeted by a vacant backyard instead of the slaphappy tail of my best friend. No one had allowed me to say goodbye, and my grief permeated a newfound loneliness.

At home, neither of my parents seemed to notice if I attended school. Semester to semester my grades fluctuated between A's and F's, a consequence of my vacillating moods and energy level. I was what I now know is called *depressed,* though I imagine there were traits of other diagnoses as well, such as conduct disorder and borderline personality disorder. To offset my emotional pain, I injured myself through punches to my face and cuts to my arms and legs. Had I been braver, I told myself, I would have finished the job, and this perceived weakness infuriated me almost as much as the thread of hope did that kept me clinging to life. Most nights I went to bed with my mind springing back and forth as if a bungee jumper at the mercy of his landing spot, eventually falling asleep exhausted from my incessant failed attempts to find solace.

Halfway through my sophomore year, my level of functioning deteriorated to an inability to get out of bed. After days with no improvement my mother took me to the family doctor, who recommended I see a psychiatrist. For unknown reasons, this never occurred. Confronting problems in our family was not a priority, and without any explanation for my ailing emotional state, I surrendered to self-blame. The first culprit was my appearance.

I hated my body. At my heaviest, I swelled to one hundred and forty-five pounds, a weight that demanded a size eleven dress for my five-foot-four frame. The plumpness on my cheeks, upper arms, and waist were obvious signs to me that I wasn't worthy of happiness. Food had become the highlight of my life and numerous attempts at dieting failed. Pimples added to my disgust, confirming that I was just as ugly outside as I felt inside. I spent much of my energy trying to find a remedy, including popping them, sitting under a sun lamp, and applying ointments, but nothing seemed to help. While most teenagers go through a period of blemishes, my distress over even one pimple on my face was so intense that I wouldn't want to leave home, adding to my already detached existence. I envisioned the entire world staring at me and laughing. Sometimes I covered them up with bandages, pretending to be injured. Other times I used artificial makeup, though the color rarely matched my skin and it hardened and cracked as if drought-ridden soil. In an attempt to go unnoticed, I walked with my head down and shoulders hunched, a stance that started in grade school and later developed into poor posture and numerous back ailments. Attending a high school where everyone knew one another and where one's appearance augmented popularity, I'm sure I was the brunt of many jokes, though I guess I was fortunate not to hear any of them.

Without Mike, one of my mother's cats adopted me. He was a large orange and white male who knew how to play fetch. Truth be known, we probably got along because he acted more like a dog. I named him Ferguson after a boy I knew. Tom Ferguson was also a loner. Dark and handsome, though not so tall as I remember, his smile lit up a room. Although we talked nearly every night on the phone

The author at fifteen years old with Ferguson

and hung out around and after school, I never really knew much about him. Perhaps we were comfortable in each other's company for that reason. Tom never questioned my attire or my mood and I never inquired how he felt or why he hung out with me. A kindred spirit of sorts, Tom was the closest thing to a friend I had for years. Then one day he disappeared. Ironically, Ferguson the cat vanished about the same time. A couple of years later I opened the newspaper and read about Tom's death in an automobile accident.

Estranged from Dana and Tess, who were now absorbed in typical high school fanfare, and with Mike, Tom, and Ferguson gone, my depressive symptoms escalated to include muteness. Implausibly, I attended high school without anyone detecting my lack of sound. At home, the typical disengagement permitted my quietness to go unnoticed as well. Despite dressing in blue jean overalls every day with my long blond hair tucked up under my baseball cap while sporting cuts and bruises on my body, I had succeeded at becoming invisible.

Some relief came my junior year when one of my teachers took an interest in me. As with Mr. B in fifth grade, I innately began looking at him as a father figure, the first since Dana's uncle during seventh grade summer. Tormented by my obsession with death, I called him nearly every night in hopes he could calm my impulsivity, though I kept him ignorant to the depth of my distress. On the nights he didn't answer, I let the phone ring and ring and ring until he got home, this being before answering machines and cell phones. Our conversations lacked candidness due to my inability to put words to my feelings, but I imagine my silence told its own story. For me, my phone calls were more about someone spending time with me than about seeking help. Due to his worry, however, my teacher eventually called my mother. For weeks, I waited optimistically for her to say something, but only silence followed. At sixteen years old, I felt abandoned, as if emancipated via parental non-participation. Without any other explanation for how I arrived at such a place, my only conclusion was that I was crazy; it seemed logical.

Visualize yourself in a foreign country unable to speak the language and your life dependent on acquiring heart medicine. How might you attempt to communicate this, to whom, and how long would it take someone to interpret your predicament? Though this task might prove challenging, your life experience, knowing what you need, and a fully developed adult brain from which to problem-solve works to your advantage. Now consider the flailing, screaming, crying youngster who just threw himself to the ground in frustration. Is this child's message, "Look at me! I'm acting this way because I want to annoy you?" or "Look at me! I need you to help me figure out what's wrong!"

I will say it bluntly. *Children act out for a reason.* Contrary to what is often popular belief, rarely do children act out because they want to make their parents angry or because they are bad seeds. The reason is as simple and as complicated as this: *Children act out because one of their needs, whether perceived or real, is unmet.* This does not negate the fact that a child acting out can look similar to a mini-devil taking revenge or an eye-rolling alien on a mission of destruction. If one can get past the presentation, however, valuable information awaits interpretation. My act of throwing spit wads at Ms. Elephant – I really *can't* remember her name – had little to do with the actual act. My behavior resulted from the unresolved emotions of feeling unloved, unwanted, and unworthy. After years of my father ignoring my needs in lieu of his own desires, I simply sought attention where I could find it, even if the attention was negative. Had someone taken the time to translate my actions, a remedy for my unmet needs may have prevented further acting out. Instead, my behaviors intensified, ultimately burying the unmet need and adding to my negative self-image by branding me rebellious, rude, out-of-control, and eventually, emotionally unstable.

👢. *Exercise 5a: Think of a time you acted out. What were the circumstances? What did you do? Try to remember how you felt. What was the outcome? Write a short summary on your timeline.*

The expression *acting out* is actually a fascinating term when examined. Think about the following: if an infant cries for attention, the parents might say, "Oh, look, the baby needs something." At this point, whatever the baby is crying about is a *need,* perhaps food, a diaper change, or snuggles. Or when a one year old uses syllables with artistic freedom in the midst of a rant, the parents might look at each other, smile, and say, "I have no idea what he wants, but isn't he cute using his words?" Then, intrigued by the pending guessing game, they try to figure out the child's need. Still, however, they view the verbal demonstration as a legitimate part of child development and not *acting out.* So, when does *acting out* become something that is viewed as negative and for which many children receive punishment? More importantly, what makes parents stop attempting to define the need behind such behaviors?

My observation has been this: at some point, most parents expect their children to know how to ask for what they need. While on the surface this seems logical, it is, unfortunately, not realistic. I mean, how many adults do you know who always ask honestly, respectfully, and directly for what they need? My point exactly. Children have an even more difficult time due to their lack of life experience and undeveloped brain. Thus, children need parental support in both understanding and acquiring their needs. Without this nurturance and guidance, *acting out* is bound to occur.

One of the mistaken assumptions around *acting out* behavior is that it is always an outward, destructive act. Many of us might envision a three-year-old child at the grocery store screaming, "I hate you!" all the while stomping his feet and turning into the likes of a wet noodle as the mother attempts to pick him up. While some children resort to this type of outward verbal and physical aggression, others yield to less obvious *acting out* behaviors such as silence, isolation, and regression. I once worked a case involving a five-year-old boy who curled up in a fetal position and rocked back and forth while sucking his thumb in the corner of his classroom. This might have been an appropriate self-soothing behavior for a much younger child, but for this boy it was a clear regression. While visiting with the child's parents, they informed me that the boy recently mutilated a cat and left it on the family's dining room table to bleed to death. My first *red flag* about this situation was that this family had not already sought help, as killing an animal is clearly an unhealthy behavior at any age. The second *red flag* unveiled itself when I went to their residence for our first therapy session to find them gone, apparently fleeing the state due to legal issues. One of my more disturbing cases, I still think about the little boy and wonder if he ever got the help he so obviously needed.

🥾 *Exercise 5b: Before moving on, think of as many 'acting out' scenarios as you can remember from your childhood and add them to your timeline at the approximate age they occurred. As you think of more over time, add them as well.*

When I became a foster parent some years ago, the value of understanding *acting out* behaviors became even more evident to me.

Because foster parents usually receive little information on a child's past, *acting out* can reveal vital clues regarding the child's unmet needs. One of my foster daughters, for example, rebelled at doing homework. After much discussion and observation, I realized her unmet needs included a lack of time management skills, understanding the purpose of homework, and knowing she had someone to count on for support. Although she was in junior high school, she had missed some important lessons due to moving around so much.

Acting out demonstrates a frustration over feeling powerlessness. My retreat to silence, for example, stemmed from not knowing how else to respond to a chronically overwhelming, dysfunctional environment. On your trail ride, learning to discover the reasons behind your acting out behaviors, as well as any behavior that is not working in your best interest, will assist you in defining your *guk*.

Exercise 5c: As you read about different childhood needs in the next few chapters, go back to your list of acting out incidents and see if you can define the missing need. In other words, why were you acting out?

A child attempting to get a need met often takes meandering paths, making the identity of the need subtle. I did not go up to my father at four years old, for example, and say, "Dad, I need to feel that you love me and want me." Rarely are needs expressed that candidly by children. Instead, I played with his stamps. Children's actions also lack premeditation. In other words, I did not consciously plan how I was going to gain my father's attention. Only as an adult with analytical skills and knowledge of child development can I look back and understand why I did what I did. The acts of children to get their needs met are actually quite remarkable and creative. Somewhere deep inside the human psyche lurks a drive so powerful that children allow others to inflict pain upon them in pursuit of getting their needs met. Such was a case I remember where a little girl acted out routinely to the point her mother would beat her. Ultimately, we discovered this was the only time she was ever touched, depicting the depth of our human need for connection, even if unhealthy.

🥾. *Exercise 5d: Consider what you would do if you were five years old, hungry, and had no one to give you food. Come up with at least five options you might try in order to avoid starvation.*

When I did this exercise, my thought process went something like this: I might first ask a neighbor for food, then a stranger, perhaps steal from a grocery store, look in the garbage, eat bugs, and somewhere along the way, I would probably throw a big tantrum. My point: some needs are relentless. True needs associated with physical or emotional health, such as food and belonging, don't disappear if they aren't met. My need for a father, for instance, followed me to adulthood. Over the years, I attempted to fill this void through both indirect and unhealthy means because I lacked the awareness that my emptiness was due to an unmet childhood need.

Okay, so you may be thinking this chapter seems more like a parenting guide than *what's my childhood got to do with it?* And that's a valid observation. Understanding childhood development from an adult, or parental, perspective is important because it heightens your awareness about any unresolved, unquestioned, or misunderstood experiences from your childhood. This, in turn, allows you to separate *healthy* experiences from *unhealthy* ones. If you didn't know children *need* food, for example, you wouldn't realize that not feeding a child is *unhealthy*. Nor might you consider hunger as a possible reason for a child to act out. Realizing that children require certain needs growing up in order to achieve healthy adulthood allows you to question if any of your childhood needs are missing, damaged, or misplaced. This, in turn, gives you an opportunity to problem-solve any areas of concern. In other words, unless you know what *should* occur in healthy development, you can't pinpoint insufficiencies.

Earlier I said children act out because one of their needs, whether perceived or real, is unmet. I want to explore that a moment. Children don't differentiate between needs and wants well. (Actually, some adults don't do this well either, but that's another book.) One important factor comes into play when trying to make sense of childhood needs. Does the acting out behavior constitute an unmet *need* or an unmet *want*? Imagine looking at your childhood and remembering a time when you wanted a cookie but ended up on the ground kicking and screaming when your 'mean' mother wouldn't give you one. Given this scenario, the concern becomes whether you were acting that way because you were starving and the cookie was a *need* or if you simply *wanted* a cookie and didn't like being told *no*. If you decide the cookie was a need, then there are obviously more issues in this scenario worth analyzing. If, on the other hand, you determine the cookie was a *want,* the next step is to question the reason for the acting out behavior. *Why* did you not like being told no? *Was* there a lack of consistent rules in your home regarding eating cookies that confused you? Or perhaps something more serious was taking place and your acting out had little to do with the actual cookie and more about a greater need such as attention. Just because the initial reason for acting out might be a *want* does not mean there isn't a missing *need* underneath. I look at *acting out* behaviors as an indication that a child needs some type of guidance. Without this guidance, *guk* may develop.

I like to compare the raising of a child to healthy adult to that of building a house. The sturdiest houses are those built on a solid foundation with lumber, insulation, plumbing, and wiring that all meet building code standards. If any of these factors (needs) lack quality, the house might crack, leak, be too cold or hot, or catch fire (act out) and have difficulty providing its purpose of shelter and safety. Likewise, if your childhood has weak areas where your needs weren't met, you might grow to adulthood and feel angry, irritable, empty, broken, damaged, unsuccessful, anxious, depressed, or even defective. In turn, these deficits may materialize in the form of poor decision-making, failed relationships, substance abuse, unfulfilling jobs, poverty, depression, and unrealized dreams. As with a house, your potential depends on the quality of your construction and the remedy of any detected deficiencies.

Exercise 5e: Envision yourself from birth to five years old. I realize I pick on this age, but it's due to my love for kindergartners. They have a certain combination of innocence, intrigue, and adventure about life that would probably do us all good to remember. So, here we go. Picture the setting where you were born. Think of the home or homes you have lived in, the city or cities, birthdays, holidays, special events, your siblings, friends, and relatives, pre-school, and kindergarten if you attended. Who was your caregiver(s)? What do you look like? Describe yourself, your interests, and your talents. Summarize this information and add it to your timeline.

If you are anything like I am when I do this exercise, you are probably amazed by this unique period of life. Children are most vulnerable between the ages of zero and five. There is no other period in life when a human develops as complexly and rapidly. It is a time of wonder, curiosity, emotion, and change. It is a time of nearly total dependence on another human for basic needs. During this period the foundation for all else in life is formed. If successful, well, it's beautiful; a child possesses the necessary tools for the next stage of development. If not successful, children attempt to compensate for the missing entities their entire lives. Because our first five years are the basis for so much of our development, it makes sense that problematic behaviors later in life can often be traced back to this early period. This is an important concept to keep in mind as you ride your trail of self-discovery.

If we believe our unmet needs in childhood simply disappear when we reach adulthood, we are fooling ourselves. The *guk* we carry with us robs our energy and creates obstacles that lessen our ability to enjoy healthier pursuits. The key word here is *needs*. They aren't called *desires* for a reason.

CHAPTER FIVE

Trail Notes

- U Children act out because one of their needs, whether perceived or real, is unmet

- U Underneath the acting out behavior lies an important message

- U Unmet needs do not disappear with adulthood

- U Raising a child is similar to building a house – each stage requires quality construction

- U Discovering unmet needs will help you find your *guk*

In memory of Holly Marino, 1964-2009,
A guardian angel to neglected, unwanted, and injured horses — and my friend.

Chapter Six
Growing Up is Hard to Do
Attachment and Development

Until the spring of my junior year, I had not participated in any typical acts of teenage curiosity such as sex, smoking, drugs, or drinking. Despite my inner turmoil, I dreamed of meeting my *one and only,* getting married, and living *happily ever after.* Of no interest to me were smoking and drugs. Alcohol, on the other hand, lured me with its easy availability and numbing effect, and parties soon served as a venue for easing a sorrow I didn't understand. This led to a series of Saturday night parties at a classmate's home with her older cousin and a few of his Army buddies from Ft. Lewis, Washington. Wearing jeans and a white hooded sweatshirt that unevenly parted my long blond hair in the back, I was bordering on painlessness when the most handsome guy I had ever seen walked over to

Brian

me and introduced himself. Immediately feeling at ease, I never looked back. Five years later, Brian and I married. At six-feet tall and 220 pounds of football physique, this funny, easygoing, and respectful guy gave me what little else could: hope.

The downside of our relationship was the five-hour separation by car and my impatience at having another year of high school to complete. I rebelled at the boundaries restricting my life, and this low tolerance soon took its toll. High on my unbearable list was Oregon's relentless rain and how dampness hung in the air like a helium balloon, leaving my toes, ears, and nose perpetually red and cold. Few could dispute that this environment's only fame came from nurturing the most loathed critter in the Northwest: the slug. Persuaded by the lack of blue sky one day, my impulsivity induced me to take the family car and drive the nearly 250 miles to Redding, California just to feel the warmth of the sun's rays on my vitamin D-starved body, having little concern over the consequences of my behavior.

Later in the year, my impetuousness surfaced again when my English teacher assigned each student a portion of Shakespeare to recite in class. Far too insecure to fathom such a display of inadequacy, I asked him if I could deliver the piece in front of him rather than the entire class. When he declined my request, I bolted similar to a racehorse through the starting gate and, by the following day, could be found hitchhiking south on Interstate 5 toward San

CHAPTER SIX

Diego. Arriving at the home of Dana's aunt and uncle, I realized that other than my fantasy of singing the blues in a smoke-filled lounge born from my idol Billie Holiday, I lacked a plan of how I was going to support myself. With no other viable options, Brian drove down from Washington to pick me up. Emotionally exhausted yet inwardly unsettled, I likened myself to one of those bouncy balls that people throw sporadically just to see where it will bounce, what it will knock into, and where it will settle. My journey ended with the familiarity of going back home, getting a job as a waitress, and picking up where life had left off, only now I had the label of *high school dropout* added to my attributes. Neither my father nor mother ever asked me why I left, gave me a lecture on the stupidity of quitting high school, or inquired what I was going to do with my life. In eighteen years, I could not remember us sharing one important conversation. I guess that's why I grew used to making all of my own decisions, even if they were lousy ones.

In no time at all, my misery returned with heightened intensity, and I again began looking at my discontent as having a physical basis. With my weight no longer a concern, I focused on my nose. Having endured nosebleeds and teasing about its crookedness since kindergarten, I secretly craved a cute, small Sally Field nose or a beautiful elegant Cybil Shepherd one. After some research, I went and saw a doctor who performed surgeries called rhinoplasty, or nose jobs, and he informed me that I had a deviated septum, the cause of my earlier nosebleeds. Naïve and lacking adequate communication skills, I apparently failed to state my intent, so after surgery when the nurse removed the bandages, the original shape of my nose remained with only my deviated septum corrected. It never crossed my mind that the doctor wouldn't fix the obvious: my nose was ugly! Embarrassed and angry, I felt even more incompetent, and my nose job became yet another topic void of conversation in our household.

My last attempt to get my father to notice me was born by my transportation needs.

Prompted by my VW bus breaking down and my father's self-professed love of motorcycles, I purchased a new blue Honda 400. Proudly calling him outside, I handed him the keys and pointed to the driveway, once again hoping for some sense of con-

The author on her motorcycle

nection. Instead, he stared at the bike a moment, then turned and walked back inside, not uttering a word. I am still unsure if that was the last time I saw my father. Shortly thereafter, my parents divorced and both moved out of our house, leaving me alone until it sold some months later.

I hadn't lived alone long before I met up with Tess and asked her to move in with me. She not only joined me as a housemate, but also began waitressing at the twenty-four-hour diner where I worked. Our reunion coincided with mutual broken hearts from her boyfriend breaking up with her and Brian ending our relationship after he left the Army and headed home to California. Consequently, Tess and I spent much of our time crying to loud, sad music. We spent another large portion of our time partying in an attempt to distract ourselves from our pain. The highlights of our existence, however, were our dogs. About a year prior, I had adopted Max, a rescue who portrayed every bit of his multi-ancestry with pride, from the intelligence of the collie, the herding instinct of the Australian shepherd, the endurance of the dingo, the protectiveness of the German shepherd, all the way to the St. Bernard freckles that made him look as though he wore a perpetual smile. In no time, Max became my loyal and attentive best friend. Feeling as though he needed a playmate, Tess acquired Wish, a sleek Irish setter that reminded me of Mike. She and Max got along extremely well and, although we took them to obedience training, they did what puppies often do best: chew. This was evident the day we came home to discover the living room ornamented from one end to the other in feathers. With the carpet barely visible, one had to look closely to find two guilty-looking mutts in the midst of their rapture. In all candidness, it may have been that Tess and I were not supreme role models. Having engaged each other in a tomato-throwing contest during one of our bereaved, drunken states, I admit it was not one of our finer moments. While I don't recall who won, I do believe the stains were still evident on the kitchen wall when the house sold.

Max

Despite this, Tess was a positive influence on me. With rather strict but loving parents, Tess had a foundation of solid morals and values and, most often, common sense. Disciplined and driven, she spent her childhood as a competitive swimmer. Though we went our separate ways after the house sold, we remained long-distance friends, participated in each other's weddings, gave birth to our first children within a month of each other, visited periodically, and lived together again some ten years later. When my life hit rock bottom, Tess was the only person who offered support.

Holly Marino rescued horses for a living. When she learned of Absolute Appeal needing a home after an injury ended his racing career, she didn't hesitate to bring him to her stable. Not long thereafter, I received a phone call. "I have a horse that might interest you." Since he'd been sired by a well-respected stud with over two-hundred offspring and earnings exceeding two million dollars, I wondered how a horse with such potential ended up on the road to slaughter. As I walked up to his paddock, my heart sank as I saw an underweight,

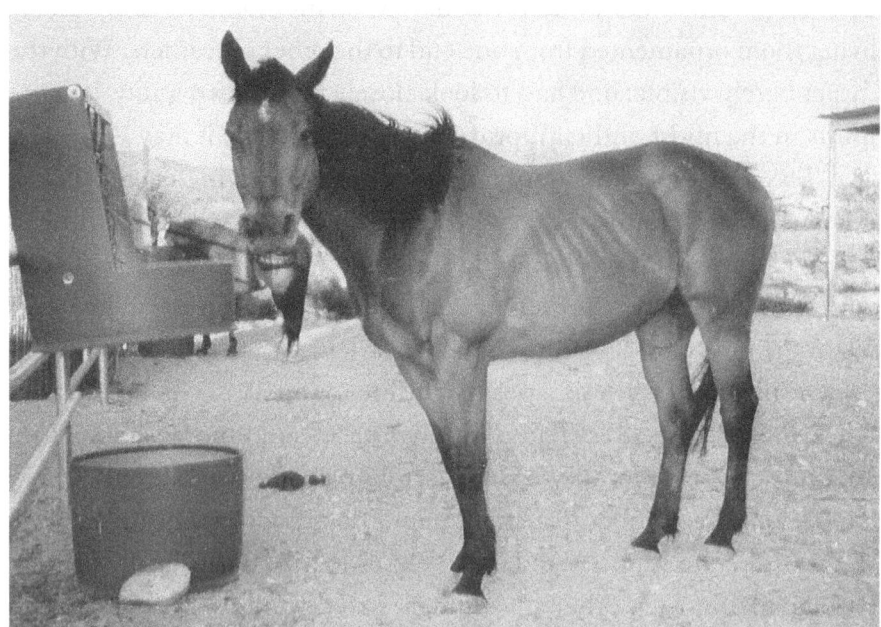

Absolute Appeal at time of rescue

lethargic horse with cuts and scars all over his body, masking his flawless conformation to the amateur eye. Though he ignored my presence, I related to him immediately. He mimicked my childhood experience: so emotionally damaged he had shut out the world. By that afternoon, Absolute Appeal was in my pasture.

Abbers, as I nicknamed him, tried to bite me when I brushed him, kicked at me when I picked up his feet, and butted me with his head if I got in his way. I characterized his behavior as *acting out*. Abber's past had been about performance, and when he no longer produced an income, someone discarded him as though he were yesterday's pizza box. Many ex-race horses, I learned, don't wind up as *lucky* as Abbers. Ferdinand, winner of the 1986 Kentucky Derby, ended up in a Japanese slaughterhouse, a fact that still leaves me outraged.

Each day for over a year I walked out to my pasture and, as if a hurt, detached child, Abbers watched me out of the corner of his eye, remaining aloof, yet keenly aware of my every move. At grooming time, my attempts to catch him imitated the likes of one-sided *tag*, often resulting in apple bribes just so I could brush him. As I tended to his injuries, I told him what a special horse he was and, occasionally, I was able to sneak in a few snuggles. Slowly, his wounds healed and he began putting on weight, although it seemed the better he felt physically, the more strength he had to demonstrate his distaste for my presence. At one point I accepted the reality that if this was as good as it got, he would simply be my 1,200-pound pet – safe, at least, from any more suffering. Then, one morning as I started my ritual in the pasture, instead of having to catch him, Abbers walked up to me, placed his muzzle on my chest, and gave me a restrained push, a gesture I interpreted as the equivalent of a gang member saying *good morning*. From there our relationship blossomed, and two years later he won reserve champion in a show division called *hunters under saddle*, the culmination of my childhood dream. In retirement, Abbers lived a leisurely life of trail rides, grazing, and unlimited snuggles. And, of course, each day he greeted me with an over-zealous nudge, right up until his death about the time I completed this book.

Abbers demonstrated the power of the work I believe in: that which is learned can be unlearned. Not a mean horse by nature, Abbers responded with anger to an environ-

The author and Abbers winning a blue ribbon

ment oblivious to his emotional needs, the similarity to children compelling. When treated with kindness and respect, however, his acting out subsided and his desire for connection returned.

With humans, the desire and ability to relate begins at birth with something called *attachment,* a concept studied by developmental psychologists Bowlby and Ainsworth. Through eye contact, expressions, verbalizations, and physical touch, a parent's first job is communicating with the child in a healthy manner in order to secure this connectedness. *Attachment founds all of a child's relationships*. Consider that statement. This is huge. In essence, successful attachment allows us the ability to bond with others. This early developmental *need* of attachment accentuates the power entrusted to parents, as the outcome of this one need alone affects every aspect of a child's life.

Imagine asking your boss a question about how to do something. The next day you are doing the task the way he wanted and he reprimands you for doing it wrong and tells you to do it a different way. The next day you do it the way he most recently asked and he reprimands you again and tells you to do it yet a different way. Now consider your frustration and confusion when this continues for a year, each day not knowing what his response will be. Would you feel secure in your relationship? Would you trust your boss? Probably not. Your advantage is having the option to speak up and point out the inconsistency in his behavior and the confusion it is causing you. You also have the choice to leave your job. Babies don't have these options. Babies are defenseless to their parents' behavior, yet have to live with the consequences.

When communication is ambiguous, a baby's perception of the world becomes confused, causing an increase in stress responses such as fear and anxiety. In turn, this compromises the development of trust and self-esteem. Inadequate attachment can result in a pendulum of outcomes, though at the severe end are the psychopaths you see depicted in the movies as void of empathy and guilt, making them fearless and coldhearted. The importance of healthy attachment cannot be over-emphasized.

I once worked with a well-meaning couple who failed to provide secure attachment due to ignorance. They believed that picking up their crying baby each time she cried would spoil the infant. As a result, they often let the baby cry and cry and cry. Other times, when they judged the crying as serious, they held the baby. With education, the couple learned that randomly choosing when to soothe and when not to soothe sent conflicting messages to their baby. After becoming more consistent in how they responded to their baby's crying, they realized a huge difference, commenting that they not only were able to figure out what the baby wanted with less difficulty, but also that the baby didn't seem to cry as much. In essence, they were communicating more effectively with their infant, allowing the creation of healthy attachment.

Parenting is similar to riding a horse. Well, what did you expect? When I taught riding lessons, I could, for the most part, get on one of the horses and get them to do what I asked. This was simply because

I had the knowledge to understand the problem. Beginner riders are often unaware of the cues their bodies give, such as the time a young student asked in frustration, "Why won't the horse move?" to which I answered, "Because you're telling the horse to stop by how tight you're holding your reins." Horse training, like parenting, has a lot to do with healthy, effective communication. The horse in the prior example was doing exactly what the rider asked even if it wasn't what the rider wanted. Children aren't that different. And this is how a myriad of unhealthy behaviors develop in children. In other words, the solution to the prior problem wasn't about *fixing* the horse; it was about educating the rider.

If you are a sports fan tired of my horse analogies, I'll say it this way: a family is comparable to a team, and the outcome of the game is contingent on the coach's play-calls. Or, for you who appreciate bluntness, let me put it this way: a child rarely gets to a place of unhealthiness without parental help, whether the parent is an active accomplice or an avoidant spectator. Now, while this may sound like blame, my objective is to convey the tremendous power parents possess over their children – power that can be utilized either positively or negatively.

Attachment is just one of many important topics of child development that will help you analyze and understand your past. A theory by Abraham Maslow also helps put healthy and unhealthy emotional growth into perspective. Maslow believed that children must have certain needs met in order to achieve other advanced needs. As you read Maslow's five levels of needs, consider the role each played in your childhood:

1) Biological (food, water, sleep, shelter),
2) Safety (free from harm),
3) Social (love, relationships, belonging, family),

4) Esteem (achievement, reputation, self-respect), and
5) Self-actualization (personal growth and fulfillment).

Biological needs such as food, water, and sleep may seem simplistic given that most of us take them for granted, but young children depend upon their caregivers for these needs. Consider the little boy I worked with in Head Start whose uncle had him sleep in his truck at night while he made deliveries. The school called me to observe this little boy because he kept falling asleep during class, an obvious interference with his learning. The problem was relatively simple, at least in theory: the boy wasn't getting enough sleep with all the truck's starts and stops. Resolving the problem became challenging, however, because the uncle called the boy a "troublemaker" for complaining and didn't want to change anything he was doing. Another child I assessed was a little girl who easily got distracted no matter what activity I attempted. As I prepared to evaluate her attention deficit, she told me she was hungry. I asked her what she had for breakfast and she told me she hadn't eaten since the day before. No wonder she couldn't concentrate! I had overlooked a basic need. This is also the reason for the establishment of free breakfast and lunch programs in the public school systems. Hunger undermines our ability to achieve higher functioning behavior.

Maslow also believed in order for other phases of healthy development to occur that children need to feel safe. Consider the three-year-old girl I worked with who got plenty of sleep and enough to eat, but who went home to a father who periodically sexually molested her. Near the end of the school day, this little girl became withdrawn. When the teacher and I investigated, we discovered the abuse and called Child Protective Services. Even though she was safe at Head Start, she feared what might happen when she got home and this overwhelmed her ability to function healthily while at school.

🥾 *Exercise 6a: Take a few minutes to write down Maslow's five levels of needs on your timeline.*

The children in the examples above were unable to achieve healthy social relationships (level 3) because they lacked biological (level 1) or safety needs (level 2). Any time a child is chronically preoccupied with one of these basic needs, healthy development has the potential to suffer. I view Maslow's theory as being applicable throughout life, and that people often go back and forth between phases. In other words, individuals who become homeless or hungry later in life may also have difficulty in achieving goals that are more advanced. For the purpose of your trail ride, Maslow's theory allows you insight into reasons for your childhood behaviors and clarity of some of the obstacles that may have blocked your path to authenticity.

A theorist named Erik Erikson also looked at conflict that arises for children during various developmental stages. These stages are helpful in understanding one's childhood because they show what can happen when needs go unmet during certain periods. In level 1, for example, a healthy environment between birth and two years old produces trust, while an unhealthy environment might produce mistrust. Here are Erikson's five levels of development:

1) Trust vs. Mistrust (birth to two years old),
2) Independence vs. Shame and Doubt (two to three years old),
3) Initiative vs. Guilt (three to five years old),
4) Industry vs. Inferiority (six to eleven years old), and
5) Identity vs. Role Confusion (twelve to eighteen years old).

🥾 *Exercise 6b: Add Erikson's stages to your timeline for easy reference. These, along with Maslow's five levels of needs from exercise 6a, will help you to see the bigger picture of*

CHAPTER SIX

development as well as how these theories complement each other in child development.

Even though most of us can't recall events prior to the age of three or four, looking at your earliest behaviors allows for insight. When I look at myself at around the age of five, I remember a child who felt shame, doubt, anxiety, fear, and guilt, and who didn't trust anyone except Mike, our dog. These are not healthy characteristics of a child in kindergarten. As an adult attempting to understand my development, Maslow and Erikson's theories help me to see where deficits in my emotional growth complicated my further development. By finding your deficits, you then have the opportunity to increase your understanding of the missing, damaged, and misplaced puzzle pieces from your childhood so you can remedy your losses. In other words, the theories of Maslow and Erikson will help you with the ultimate question: "What's in *your guk* bag?"

Understanding child development enables you to make correlations between your experiences and your current behaviors. When you become aware of the reasons for your behaviors, changing them becomes more logical. This is also the foundation behind cognitive-behavioral therapy. I like thinking of it as the difference between telling a child "don't touch the stove because I said so" versus "don't touch the stove because you'll get burned." Studies show people like to know why they *should* or *shouldn't* do something. Perhaps that's why the most common question a child asks is *why?* Many children will touch the stove if not given a satisfactory reason for why they shouldn't. It has to do with the curiosity factor. If they don't understand *why*, they will find out for themselves. Discovering your past allows you to use this type of logic to differentiate your healthy behavior from your unhealthy behavior. In turn, you then have the opportunity to resolve the unhealthy behavior in order to produce a more favorable outcome.

Knowledge regarding healthy child development will help you compile your childhood story. I know what I discovered intrigued me; you may be intrigued too. Little humans are quite amazing if you take the time to understand them. This knowledge might also clear up any faulty assumptions you have about yourself or, if you are a parent, provide clarity regarding some aspect of parenthood. After all, understanding your childhood is one of the best ways to enhance your parenting skills. You got it. Knowledge is power.

Sometimes I wonder how many potential owners bypassed Abbers, viewing him only as an old, beat-up, mean horse not deserving of a second chance. Did they even consider how a once prized colt with so much promise ended up in such a drastic state? Without a doubt, the loss was theirs. Abbers became my gem. As you look back at your childhood, I urge you to bypass judgment and, instead, ask *why* in order to gain valuable insight into your life's unknown treasures. Curiosity may have killed the cat, but inquisitiveness is a tremendous asset for humans.

CHAPTER SIX

Trail Notes

- ⋃ That which has been learned can be unlearned

- ⋃ Whether healthy or unhealthy, attachment sets the stage for all else in a child's life

- ⋃ Children develop like steps, with each one dependent on the strength of the one before it

- ⋃ Asking "why?" provides insight

- ⋃ Parents who understand their childhoods have more insight into parenting

Chapter Seven

The Greatest Organ of All

Personality or Temperament

Looking back, I probably should have foreseen the downfall of my relationship with my oldest sister. Like so often occurs in unhealthy homes, the dysfunction of the environment that once brought us closer, ultimately tore us apart. Having offered to stay at her and her husband's home to help care for their ill baby so she could get some sleep, I was rocking the infant in the wee hours of the morning when an inebriated family member walked in and made unwelcome sexual advances. Though my sister awakened and came in the room when I yelled, she failed to stand up for me and I left, the incident forever damaging our already frail relationship.

When our family home sold soon thereafter, I couldn't get out of town fast enough. My first stop was a Morgan horse ranch about thirty miles north where I took a job as a stable hand. In a landscape of rolling green hills scattered with sheep and horses, I was in my element, and for room and board I fed, watered, and groomed the family's three pregnant mares. It was here I purchased Thunder, the ex-barrel racer, after seeing him grazing in a nearby pasture. The matron of the farm was a kind woman with four beautiful daughters, none of whom had an interest in horses, a concept that left me bewildered. After the mares foaled, I became restless and an inner drive convinced me it was time to move on. I was looking for something, though I had no idea what that *something* was. With Max and Thunder in tow, I headed northward yet again in search of a more promising future.

My next stop was Sauvie Island, a community located northwest of Portland nestled between the Willamette and Columbia Rivers, and home to numerous varieties of waterfowl during their migratory season. With few skills, I began work for the Oregon Department of Fish and Wildlife clearing walking trails for wildlife viewers. This temporary position turned into two-plus years, a boatload of education, and a new father figure. Frank, my boss, taught me about waterfowl, planting crops, and driving a tractor. I spent as much time with him as possible, delighting in feeling as though I was his daughter. He allowed me to live in a small cabin on the banks of Sturgeon Lake, complete with an outhouse and within walking distance to a stocked trout pond and wild blackberries that offered abundant jam makings. Adjacent to the cabin sat a big old red barn where Thunder lived with at least one vocal barn owl, numerous mice, and an occasional possum. Max savored the island unleashed where the nearest house was beyond eyesight, quickly forging a love-hate relationship with an equally energetic squirrel. Running ahead of the truck as I headed to work each morning, Max detoured into a certain field to chase what I assumed was the same squirrel up a large lone oak tree. Day after day, I watched with anticipation to see if he caught the squirrel, but each day the chase ended in the same manner with the squirrel running up the tree leaving a barking Max circling at the bottom. Then one day as usual, Max ran into the field. Instead of running away, however, the squirrel remained still, leaving

CHAPTER SEVEN

The author's cabin on Sauvie Island

the two of them nearly nose-to-nose staring at each other. So startled when he realized what was happening, Max froze in disbelief, giving the squirrel time to get away. Only when the squirrel was a safe distance did he begin his chase and allow the ritual to continue. After jumping into the truck to continue our journey, Max just looked at me with his ever convincing smile as if to say, *Well, if I had caught him today, what fun would I have had tomorrow?*

Thunder's barn on Sauvie Island

During hunting season my mornings began outside, rain or shine, with my soaped-up head upside down under my primary water source, an old army tanker filled with incredibly cold water. I then headed to the field station to assist checking hunters in for waterfowl season or to search

The author collecting dead waterfowl

for dead birds for study, a welcome change from my regular job duties. One of the men brought fresh cream from his cow for our coffee and we passed the time waiting for hunters by playing cribbage. Although welcomed by the other workers, my anxiety kept me from feeling as though I belonged, and I soon realized I simply didn't know how to fit into the world for which I hungered.

Living on the island provided solitude, and although there was a normalcy about being by myself, an unbearable loneliness ensued. I reluctantly went on a few blind dates set up by well-intentioned co-workers, but my heart would not close the door on Brian. In time, instead of forcing myself to socialize, I stayed at home and hiked with Max or explored the island on horseback. It was on one of these expeditions that I watched Mount St. Helens erupt across the river, the ash covering our island and leaving a distasteful grit whenever the wind blew.

Twice a month I left the safety of my remote existence to drive the twenty-some miles to the nearest laundromat on the seedier outskirts of

Mount St. Helens erupting

CHAPTER SEVEN

Portland. Arriving at the desolate little building late one Friday night, I was about to put the coins in the washing machine when a dirty, unshaven, and scary looking man approached me making rude and suggestive comments. Before I could react, Max poked his head around the corner and growled, his jaw dripping saliva and trembling with anticipation. The man, apparently not a dog person, turned and left, and it was some time before I realized my lack of good judgment. Thankfully, I had inherited a protector in Max, a position otherwise void in my life.

As my job on the island concluded, my dream of working with horses materialized when I learned of my acceptance to a riding school in California. At about the same time, Brian came back into my life and we became engaged. Our marriage ceremony occurred in the only church on the island via a candlelight service with Frank giving me away after failing to receive word from my father regarding his intended participation. After a honeymoon in Canada, Brian and I headed to California, I for the dormitories of

The author's wedding day

horse school, and Brian to his prior job near San Jose. We lived about three hours apart and saw each other on weekends.

I had been at horse school less than a month when Brian came to let me know my father had died. For reasons still unclear to me, my mother chose to tell Brian rather than me and did so after the funeral, not allowing me the option of attending. Unaware of my father's failing health, the incident left me feeling further alienated from my family. In the end, the news of my father's death gave finality to my childish fantasy that he would one day come looking for me, wanting to know his daughter. In truth, his death changed little in my life. I had missed my father for as long as I could remember.

Stifling any emotion that attempted to surface, I forced myself to concentrate on the challenges of school where I was learning to become an instructor for a type of horse training called *hunters and jumpers*. With most of my classmates being avid riders since early childhood, I struggled to keep up, both mentally and physically.

The author at horse school

Lacking problem-solving skills, I discovered my strongest survival tactics of hiding or running away worked against my success. Horse school asked of me what felt unfamiliar and out of reach, and although I completed my training and accepted a job at a stable in the State of Washington, I felt as though I was an impostor. Instead of feeling successful for having reached my goal, I questioned if I was chasing something mystical that was out of my reach.

Fact: The three pounds of brain in your head is the most fascinating piece of machinery on Earth. Without it, you aren't *you*. Damage it and you aren't *you*. But understand it to the best of your ability, and you will gain unprecedented power over your life.

Once upon a time scientists believed that the circumference of one's head determined sanity. Today, after additional research, experts agree that both nature and nurture play a role in emotional development, making one's head size irrelevant unless buying a hat. We now understand that dismissing the influence of one's environment defies logic, the same as if we ignored the fact that every person is born with some predetermined characteristics. Also amiss would be to think we know everything about the brain. As easy as it is to believe that science is all fact, most of science consists of theories, hypotheses, or mysteries. Still today, researchers don't agree on the Earth's origin, why we sleep, or even if Bigfoot truly exists. What does that mean for us? Let me put it this way: like science, learning about oneself is an infinite process. If tomorrow, for example, I learned I was the resurrection of Epona, the Gallo-Roman Goddess of horses, I would need to incorporate that new piece of information into my current understanding of myself. So far, however, I haven't heard that one, although it may explain a lot.

As you begin to question why you believe and behave as you do, the benefits are numerous. And when these questions become routine, your inquiries begin to feel natural, similar to driving the same route to work each day. In time, your mind asks the questions without prompting, as though on autopilot. At this point in my life, I have difficulty *not* labeling my behavior as either healthy or unhealthy and *not* looking for a reason behind my actions. Some call this process *self-actualization,* a term that Maslow used for the pursuit of realizing and achieving one's greatest potential. I look at the process of self-actualization as a way of life, perhaps similar to how I see my profession of therapy: to be receptive to new information so that I arrive at the most accurate results. Regardless of your age, there is never a time in your life when you aren't changing. Have you ever heard the saying, *The only constant in life is change?* This means you are playing *catch-up* right now. Once you process your *guk* from the past, you will have a clean slate. Then all you have to do is take one day at a time and resolve *guk* as it develops so it doesn't have a chance to accumulate. In essence, you will be able to live in the present and plan a healthier future because you understand your past.

To help you reach this goal of finding and removing your *guk,* there are two terms worthy of understanding: temperament and personality. Many people use these terms interchangeably, though they are actually quite different. So let's get started.

Like snowflakes, we all enter the world unique. From the moment of conception, you were destined to have certain physical and mental characteristics. Your height, eye color, and body type make up some of these physical characteristics. Likewise, you also have one-of-a-kind mental characteristics called *temperament,* a topic we will define a little later. As with your physical traits, your temperament will not change over the course of your lifetime. Your *personality*, in comparison, *can* change, and I like to think of personality as the result of how your temperament interacts with your environment. An easy way to remember it is this way: if you were a house, your temperament would be the cement foundation (constant) and your personality would be the furnishings in the house (changeable).

Consider your temperament for a moment. Again, you can't change your temperament except perhaps with the help of a neurosurgeon, although this isn't my recommendation. There are numerous theories about what attributes make up one's temperament and they are well worth the research if you are interested. For our purposes, I have chosen four traits that most scientific realms consider valid. They include:

1) your interests and talents,
2) your learning style,
3) your energy cycle, and
4) whether you are an extrovert or an introvert.

Interests/Talent: I didn't learn to love horses; I was born with a love for horses. While interests can strengthen with exploration, exploration will not necessarily facilitate interest. Talent is similar. Some people have talent, but their environment doesn't allow for its development. Would Michael Jordan be famous if he never played basketball? Would anyone know of his talent? Unless there is opportunity, who knows what talents lurk inside any of us. On the other hand, unlimited opportunity won't make a difference if you don't have talent. Case in point: my musical aptitude. I had access to two musicians (my grandparents), yet no amount of practice would've made me a concert pianist. My potential in other musical realms was equally grim, including singing and playing the trombone, clarinet, guitar, and cello. I even like to think I would've had enough insight not to try out for *American Idol* had it been around, ultimately shielding me from Randy's, "Oh, Dawg…, really?"

Learning Style: If you are like most people, you are probably dominant in one of the three learning styles: auditory, visual, and kinesthetic. Auditory learners retain information best through hearing the words. They listen to verbal expression and take into account the tone and pitch of one's voice. In grade school they are the students who love to read aloud or ask questions; in college they tape lectures. Visual learners, on the other hand, take notes, look at life in picture-form, and sit in the front of the classroom. Kinesthetic learners like *doing* things. They tend to explore, engage in hands-on activities, and are not content sitting still for long periods watching or listening.

Energy Cycle: You've probably heard someone say, "I'm a night person" or "I'm most productive in the morning." What they are talking about is their energy cycle. While it's not rocket science to know that people do best when they maintain a consistent routine, get enough sleep, and eat well, sometimes we don't think about what time of day we are most alert and productive and what time of day we begin to fade and lose energy. My oldest son, Gabe, is a morning person, as am I. When he was growing up, we both rose early and got a lot of work done. When my youngest son, Zach, woke up, or should I say when I woke him up, he drudged around and sighed at our cheeriness. Come evening, however, Zach's enthusiasm revealed itself while Gabe and I melted into the couch for some relaxation. Knowing your strengths and weaknesses gives you yet another tool with which to make the best decisions for your life.

Extrovert/Introvert: About three-fourths of people are extroverts and the other fourth are introverts. Consider which you are as I describe the differences: extroverts tend to talk before they think and re-energize when around people. Introverts, conversely, tend to think before they talk and need to be alone to re-energize. Wherever you fall on the introvert/extrovert scale, awareness of your position is vital to understanding some of your behaviors and feelings. If you are a solid introvert and work as a car salesperson, for example, it might make sense if you dread going to your job. Having to not only talk to people all day but also try to sell them something could take a lot of energy and aptitude that introverts don't have. Likewise, if you are an extrovert and work as a data entry person, you might be unhappy in your job because you don't get to use your innate outgoing desire to be around people. Taking into consideration whether you are an introvert or an extrovert when you look at your childhood experiences can provide additional insight.

Exercise 7a: Write down the four characteristics of your temperament. For example, I am an introvert, a morning person, a kinesthetic/visual learner, my interests include horseback riding, animals, classical music, and human behavior, and two of my talents are making cinnamon rolls and scrapbooking.

Keeping in mind that you have a one-of-a-kind, consistent temperament, let's now look at personality. As stated previously, your personality is the result of how your temperament interacts with your ever-changing world. This means your personality is molded by numerous factors, including your parents, family, friends, school, religion, travel, beliefs, values, trauma, abuse, dysfunction, past experiences, future goals, deaths, accidents, movies, video games, food, and physical health. You got it – everything. This also means the healthiness or unhealthiness of your environment has a direct impact on the development of your personality, especially as a child when you have little control. As I mentioned earlier, my personality growing up became so unstable that I called myself *personality-less* because I didn't feel I had any consistent characteristics. All my behaviors and feelings felt reactive instead of resulting from a place of stability. Again, the power of parents and our environment on our emotional health is greatly underestimated.

Have you ever known anyone who *found* religion? This is a prime example of how someone's personality changes in new circumstances. Trauma, an emotional experience, and some type of enlightenment can initiate personality changes. While most personality changes are subtle, our personalities continually change with our environment and experiences. Can you think of someone you hadn't seen in awhile and when you reunited you discovered that the person seemed different? Humans are not stagnant beings. This is why understanding yourself plays an important role in your guiding your life in the direction of your choice. And as you might expect by now, this understanding begins with your childhood.

Exercise 7b: Think about all the different personality traits you have had over the years and add them to your timeline at the approximate age you remember having them. On my timeline, for example, I placed traits such as shy and quiet in my preschool area, then added devious and manipulative during grade school, depressed and suicidal in junior high school, impulsive and impatient with a hopeful optimism when I met Brian, and so on, showing both the range of traits I remember having as well as the traits I was labeled by others.

Your experiences in life, both in childhood and adulthood, have the potential to take you closer to or farther away from your healthiest, most genuine self. As you continue along your trail ride, your timeline will allow you to see what factors influenced your development. This will then allow you to find the obstacles that stand in your way of completing your puzzle and understanding your childhood story.

I had a patient once who asked me why she was so *screwed up* (her words) when her siblings seem so *normal* (again, her words). After discussing her choice of wording, our conversation brought to light the fact that, even when parents feel they treat their children all the same, different results occur. All this really means is that different temperaments create different personalities, which, in turn, react differently to similar experiences. Did you get that? Different temperaments create different personalities even in the same environment. Okay? Then, given that, these unique individuals react differently to similar experiences. Make sense? Indisputably, however, no two siblings ever really have the same experience. Even if two sisters are in the same place at the same time watching the same television show, the experience for each child will differ not only due to their individual temperaments, but also because of their past experiences, developmental age, and personality. And unless joined at the hip, most siblings have different experiences. In my family, for example, my sisters didn't go with our father on his outings. This, in and of itself, facilitated a much different childhood experience for them than for me. But even if they had gone with my father on his outings, their experiences would've materialized through their worldview, not mine.

Personality and temperament are fascinating topics that help increase our understanding of ourselves so that we have the ability to make healthier choices. If you are interested in a more in-depth understanding of yourself, I recommend taking the Myers-Briggs Type Indicator® assessment. As one of the founders, Isabel Briggs Myers stated, "Whatever the circumstances of your life, the understanding of type can make your perceptions clearer, your judgment sounder, and your life closer to your heart's desire."

Without a doubt, the brain is *the greatest organ of all.* Similar to a computer, however, we benefit most when we are able to access the most relevant and accurate data for our needs. Persevering toward the truth rather than holding on to faulty information is often the difference between success and disappointment. Such was the unexpected pleasure to Columbus when he failed to fall off the *flat* earth.

Trail Notes

- No two people interpret the same experience alike

- Learning about oneself never ends because we never stop changing

- Self-actualization is a philosophy for living life

- You are born with one lifelong temperament while your personality develops and changes throughout your life

- Understanding yourself allows you to make effective decisions about your life

Chapter Eight

Born to Be Me

Defense Mechanisms and Resiliency

My first job as a riding instructor came with the added bonuses of my employer hiring Brian as the barn manager and giving us a cottage in which to live. With twelve horses in my care I gave riding lessons, taught horse management to university students, and tended to my horse's exercising and grooming needs. While the physical aspects of the job were challenging yet achievable, I was less adept at the politics founding a show barn. After a few months, Brian and I concluded the stable was not a good fit and we headed to Texas after attempts to find jobs in the recession-hit Seattle area failed. Despite the circumstances, I found the move exciting. Still believing my next stop in life would be better than the last, the lure of the unknown bore familiarity, endorsing both my optimism for the future as well as my ignorance about my past.

Texas proved ill fated, however, when shortly after our arrival Max dug out of our yard and was hit by a car. I found him on our doorstep, and though he appeared to have no apparent injuries, his eyes said otherwise. I don't remember how I got him to the veterinarian's office or onto the sterile table, but instinctively I found myself stroking the muscular contour of his body as I had done so many times before. "Don't touch him," the assistant snipped, "he's probably in shock and will bite you." I ignored her order. Frankly, I didn't care if he bit me if that's what he needed to do. But he didn't. He just looked at me with his big brown eyes as if to say, "I tried my hardest to get home so you wouldn't have to wonder what happened to me." Knowing in my heart that this was true, I told him I loved him and thanked him for being my best friend. Then, helplessly, I laid my face aside his as he took his last breath, the veterinarian yet to enter the room. With a smile still on his face, I closed his eyes, shaming myself for thinking he could be happy in a small cedar-fenced yard after having hundreds of acres to roam freely. I attempted to avoid grieving for Max by replacing him, though I would not attach to another dog for a decade.

Not long thereafter, Thunder died due to my medical error, compounding my grief. Reverting to the likes of a traumatized five year old, I ran from the pasture to my room and lay frozen on my bed, unable to bear the pain. The reality of my childhood dream, Thunder was my first equine partner who, unhesitatingly, carried me thirty-some miles to our new home on Sauvie Island when I didn't have a horse trailer. Envisioning life without him seemed unimaginable, and not capable of facing my anguish, I submerged myself in twelve to fourteen-hour days at my job as assistant trainer at a polo club, ignoring all else.

When the recession overtook Houston, Brian and I found ourselves packing again, this time betting on his new job in Kansas to bring stability to our life. Despite our many adventures since marrying, my idealistic innocence led me to believe that our marriage was the end-all, certain that Brian and I would endure whatever life handed us. Reality, however, showed that I knew little about what a marriage took to succeed. The extent of my communication deficits included total avoidance to writing notes rather than speaking to Brian in person. Yet even that took courage. My behavior did not result from a lack of trying; I simply didn't know how to express feelings that were muddled in layers of *guk*. A product of my past, I was naïve, impulsive, easily frustrated, and void of the tools necessary for healthy adult functioning, particularly an intimate relationship. My level of insight and awareness was probably that of a twelve year old, though that might be a generous assessment. Marriage allowed me someone to depend on for the first time in my life and I latched onto it, reverting to the role of a carefree child. Still craving the provisions a father provides a daughter, I unintentionally placed Brian in a role other than equal partner. Temporarily masking my shortcomings and giving me a false sense of healthiness, I unknowingly used marriage as an escape from a prison I didn't know I was locked inside. My marriage could not hide me from my torment, however, and three years later we separated, just after moving back to California with the two irrefutable highlights of our union: Gabriel Jacob, almost two, and Zachary Luke, three months.

Separating went against everything I believed in, yet I didn't know how to save our marriage. If not for Tess in Oregon offering to let us live in her basement, we would've been homeless. For reasons unclear to me, my mother denied my request to stay with her temporarily, creating even more ambiguity for me surrounding the term *family*. Nearing my emotional breaking point, I departed California with less than $200 in my purse and our two sons, both in diapers, clueless as to how I was going to survive.

Once settled at Tess's, I found myself in a position of doing what I never fathomed: filing for

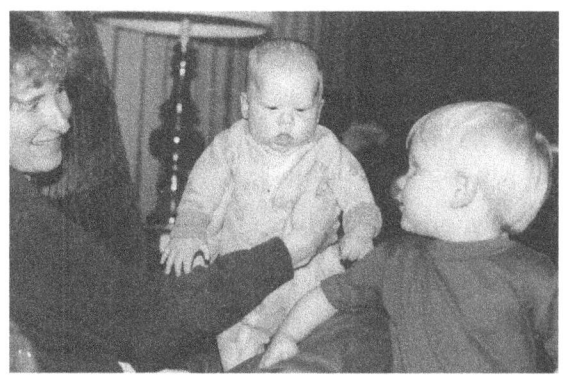

The author, Zach, and Gabe

food stamps. I have yet to find anything quite as humbling as being broke, unemployed, uneducated, and yet solely responsible for two innocent babies. Perhaps at that point in my life my immaturity was an asset, as had I realized the scope of my predicament I may have not fared as well as I did. Survival was what I knew and, instinctively, I returned to this familiarity, my armor in place. Not wanting my marriage to end, I filed only separation papers, holding on to the naïve belief that Brian and I would work things out – that he would miss me – that he would ask me to come home. Six months later with no reconciliation in sight, I reluctantly changed the paperwork to a divorce, combating my engrained belief of *till death do us part.*

Desperate to provide for my children, yet apprehensive about working at a full-time, dead end job and never seeing them, I began taking classes at a nearby community college in order to earn my high school diploma. Tess made this undertaking possible by offering to watch Gabe and Zach for a few hours each day. Surprised by my enjoyment of learning, I applied for scholarships, grants, and student loans so I could stay in college, hire a part-time babysitter, *and* do what was most important to me: spend time with my children. Going into debt seemed like a small price to pay for being able to raise my sons, a decision I have never regretted.

During the few months we lived with her, Tess became my parenting mentor. Infatuated with child development, she sold educational toys and our children reaped the benefits of playing with all the samples. Tess's love for children's books also introduced me to the importance of reading to my children, an event I incorporated into our daily routine. My prior experience with children was limited to babysitting in high school and rather short-lived at that. As I remember, the parents came home and asked if I wanted to watch their child again and I said, "No, but I would love to take your dog out for a walk sometime." And that was that. Still missing my childhood dog, Mike, I returned only to take their black Labrador to the park to play fetch. With my own children, however, I felt an immediate

CHAPTER EIGHT 113

Tess, daughter Kaila, two, Gabe, two, the author, and Zach, six months

and unbelievably poignant bond, inspiring me to learn as much as I could about parenting. Living with Tess and her husband allowed me this opportunity through witnessing a healthy family firsthand, and I attempted to integrate similar values into my parenting, such as consistency, respect, listening, boundaries, nurturing, and the concept that *anytime* is a *teachable* moment. These lessons proved invaluable to me as I faced the difficult years ahead.

I was fast asleep one night when a squeak coming from my bedroom window awakened me. Squinting toward the sound, I saw a hand reach inside the screen to unlatch my window. As if in slow motion, my mouth opened and I screamed. Unfortunately, no sound came out. Frozen in fear, my brain attempted to protect me from potential harm. I came to find out the intruder was Brian attempting not to wake me after forgetting his key. His gain, perhaps, was learning how to shut me up, though I believe the words that eventually made it out of my mouth may have offset this feat.

While flight, fight, and freeze are common reactions to physical danger, sometimes we aren't as familiar with the *defense mechanisms* that help protect us from emotional danger. Historically, Sigmund Freud defined defense mechanisms as *unconscious resources used by the ego to reduce conflict and anxiety*. Simply, they are good things that provide the brain temporary relief from bad things. The problem is, sometimes defense mechanisms overstay their welcome.

A common defense mechanism I saw day after day in my crisis work is denial. As a volunteer for our fire department's crisis response team, one of my duties was conducting death notifications to next-of-kin. When informing someone of a death, I confirmed who I was speaking to, their relationship to the deceased, and then stated the death notice. An example sounds like this:

"Are you Mrs. Doe?"

"Yes."

"Mrs. Doe, do you have a son by the name of John Doe born 2/10/88?"

"Yes."

"Mrs. Doe, I am sorry to have to inform you that your son, John, has been killed in a car accident tonight."

More often than not, the person responds with a statement such as, "No, you must be wrong." Denial. It is the brain's way of protecting a person from shock, thus allowing the information to be taken in slowly for processing.

Other defense mechanisms are not this straightforward, as when I pulled Travis' hair out in second grade. Poor Travis was simply in the wrong place at the wrong time when my anger exploded. This defense mechanism, called displacement, occurs when *an emotion is redirected from a dangerous place to a safer outlet.* In this case, releasing my anger on Travis was safer than confronting my parents, who were the actual source of my anger.

Along with denial and displacement, we use numerous additional defense mechanisms in response to stressful occurrences in our lives. Earlier in this book, for instance, I discussed my habit of dreaming of a safe place with dogs, horses, and macaroni and cheese. This type of daydreaming is not uncommon in children who live in chronically negative environments and is called *magical thinking*. Magical thinking allows a child in a powerless situation to maintain hope. I find defense mechanisms fascinating because they suggest that even when behavior appears difficult to interpret, a logical reason probably exists, even if that reason resides deep in one's psyche.

Exercise 8a: As you think about the defense mechanisms discussed in this chapter, consider if you have experienced any of them and place them on your timeline at the age you think they developed. As with any of the previous exercises, you can continue adding to your timeline as your awareness broadens.

Regression: *to revert to an earlier stage of development when faced with overwhelming stimulation.* As if in a time machine, we often return to a prior developmental period when our level of stress exceeds our ability to cope. While working on a mobile crisis unit, a number of our calls involved the removal of children from their homes due to abuse. These situations resulted in many of the upper grade school children regressing to self-soothing behaviors common in babies such as thumb sucking or rocking back and forth.

Rationalization: *to supply an alternative reason for something occurring rather than the truth.* For a long time I rationalized the reason for my failed marriage because I was unable to acknowledge my truths. Rationalization commonly replaces or prolongs accountability. The long-term harm in rationalizing is the lost opportunity to resolve the *guk* that distances you from your genuine self.

Intellectualization: *to avoid emotions by focusing on the intellectual aspect.* If an award were given for this one, I would win. Having championed the ability to hold in my emotions, intellectualizing became one of my long-term destructive defense mechanisms. My therapist eventually broke through this barrier by reiterating the phrase, "Okay, I know what you *think*, now tell me how you *feel.*" I really hated when he did this, but I'll admit it helped.

Splitting: *this defense mechanism often occurs in chronic cases of dysfunction or abuse causing the brain to view things as all good or all bad.* Due to my negative experiences growing up in Oregon, I ended up believing everything about Oregon was negative. When in an unhealthy environment, a black-and-white perspective makes life easier because it gives the impression, albeit false, of having more control. In my case, *Oregon* took the blame for my unhappiness, causing me to believe I would be happy if I left. The world, however, is rarely black and white.

Repression: *to not allow painful or dangerous memories into consciousness.* Memory issues are common in children who experience unhealthiness. I suspect I still have some repressed memories. Sometimes, discovering repressed memories can help in the healing process. Other times, not unlike beehives, disturbing traumatic memories may prove harmful. I recommend consulting a mental health professional who specializes in this area if repression is a concern.

One of the more severe defense mechanisms is disassociation: *a partial or complete interruption in the brain during the thought process.* My first awareness this might be happening with me was when my therapist had to yell my name in order to jolt me from a paralyzed stance. When

I snapped back to reality, I only remember that he had asked me a question, though I had no memory of the actual question. I imagine this type of disassociation began early in my childhood. I look at disassociation as the brain's way of blocking a memory that has the potential to cause emotional harm. Many people may recognize the term *disassociation* due to its connection to multiple personalities, a topic made famous by the movie, *Sybil*, which tells the story of psychiatrist Cornelia B. Wilbur and her studies on the controversial topic. To me, disassociation makes logical sense and is yet another indication of how the brain exerts its power in an attempt to safeguard healthiness.

Most of us unknowingly use defense mechanisms in our everyday lives. While some are needed and protect us when we are vulnerable, others may have become a part of our learned behavior and work against our well-being. Awareness is the first step to understanding the reason for utilizing any defense mechanism. Once in your awareness, you can then assess its impact on your life and work to form a healthier response. One way to gain awareness is to listen to the opinions of those close to you. You might remember your spouse complaining, "Every time I get serious you crack a joke," or a friend commenting, "Whenever I ask you how you feel you change the subject." The problem with not becoming aware of or resolving chronic defense mechanisms is that they promote the stockpiling of our *guk*. In turn, when we allow something to block our truth, we reduce our authenticity. I don't know about you, but the topics I tend to avoid are usually also the ones that I most need to resolve.

Exercise 8b: Think about the last disagreement or argument you had with someone. Take this incident and use PAS (processing a story) from exercise 3c. Now, think of two additional disagreements or arguments and do the same. How did you respond in each of the situations? Do you see any patterns in your action or non-action?

> *Arguments often provide an example of when we use a defense mechanism because emotions are high and the majority of people don't like conflict, so our defenses tend to engage. Most people also find a pattern in their behavior when it comes to conflict. Was the conflict resolved in the situations you assessed? Did you use any defense mechanisms? Do you foresee the same type of conflict arising again? Keep in mind that defense mechanisms often interfere with healthy resolution.*

Now I want to talk about something called a *trigger*. And no, for you fellow horse buffs, I'm not talking about Roy Roger's horse. A *trigger* is an internal signal from our brain that sets off a reaction. Getting into a car as a passenger, for example, sends a trigger to my brain for my anxiety to begin. Triggers can be places, words, smells, sights, feelings, or a touch. While some triggers ignite positive thoughts, such as thinking of a loved one after hearing a particular song, we are mainly concerned with invasive triggers that alert you to your *guk*. A common trigger seen on television usually depicting a war veteran is that of a car backfiring, causing the person to hit the ground for cover, thinking the sound was gunfire. I once had a patient who called her triggers *the triple "i" response*, defining the feeling of powerlessness as *impulsive, irritating, and icky,* and I could certainly relate. Triggers can feel similar to demonic possessions that overtake your body, leaving you at the mercy of your reactions. Once you acknowledge and understand your triggers, you have more power to control them through resolving the issue causing them, learning new responses, or setting firmer boundaries in order to protect yourself.

> *Exercise 8c: Make a list of both your positive and negative triggers and write them on your timeline. Add additional triggers as they come into your awareness.*

CHAPTER EIGHT

To become aware of your triggers, try to remember what you were thinking about just prior to a situation where you found yourself reacting impulsively, sometimes regretfully or with embarrassment. One of my stronger triggers is the smell of stale alcohol. This creates an immediate change in my mood to the feeling of desperate rage and I automatically visualize my father. Then I get the urge to scream, cry, and punch whatever is in my path. While I can now control these feelings because I understand them, these types of triggers dominated my existence for years. This was one of the reasons I felt out of control; I had numerous triggers governing my thoughts and behaviors.

This now brings us to the topic of resiliency. As a society, we often placate misfortune when it comes to children, speaking of their *remarkable* resiliency. "Oh, don't worry about the children, kids are resilient!" When I hear such statements, I want to shout in outrage because, more often than not, the words lack accuracy. If children were so resilient to their environments, they wouldn't need to try to escape reality through overeating, self-mutilating, bullying, taking drugs, joining gangs, or killing themselves. Neither would parents need to buy anti-depressant and anti-anxiety medications for their children. Although not always a welcome truth, children are much more vulnerable than most of us realize, and the cost to us as a society for not making our children's emotional health our highest priority is unfathomable. *Remarkably resilient* has been proven time and time again to be a myth or, at the most, an anomaly. Yes, children *do* adapt to their environments, but it commonly comes with a cost to their emotional health.

The term *resilience*, however, does pose an interesting question. Why do some children from challenging beginnings achieve success when others in similar circumstances do not? Let's first look at the definition of resilience: *the ability to recover from or adjust easily to misfortune or change*. By definition alone, some children are more resilient than others simply by their unique temperament. I once worked a prevention program where my job was to assess two to five year olds for resiliency and then attempt to teach them skills that would increase their resiliency. According to researchers, factors that improve resiliency include a sense of belonging, hope, power, and at least one adult on whom they can count. I see benefit in such work. To say blatantly that children are resilient, however, is false. Think of it this way: if an adult is struggling emotionally with consequences of childhood issues, whatever resiliency was in place at the time obviously wasn't enough. Each of us has a point at which we will suffer negative consequences from what occurs in life if we aren't resilient enough. Or, as one of my mentors used to say, "We are all but one step from insanity; we just don't know which step it might be." Okay, that's a bit harsh, but you get my point. Perhaps the ultimate message we should be taking from the topic of resiliency is this: the less need for it, the better.

Exercise 8d: What resiliency factors did you have growing up that added to your sense of belonging, hope, and power? These factors can be people, pets, places, goals, or experiences (school, hobbies, jobs, sports). Did you have at least one adult on whom you could count? Add these to your timeline.

Even though I went down many dangerous roads and made many unwise decisions in my life, I often think the end result would have been far worse had I not had certain experiences. My first protective factor was my dog, Mike. From the toddler stage on, Mike was my companion and confidant. He allowed me to feel less alone. Had he not been in my life, perhaps my degree of isolation and hopelessness would have been worse. My next resiliency factor was my friend, Dana. She distracted me from my troubles and gave me her friendship. And the list continues: my dream of owning a horse,

CHAPTER EIGHT

Tess, my teacher in high school, Tom, Ferguson, Max, Thunder, Frank, and horse school. And, of course, Brian. He entered my life just as I started to experiment a little too much with alcohol. Without his love, I question what poor decisions I might have made next. Without a doubt, however, my strongest resiliency factors have been my sons. Their ability to make me laugh and allow me to see life through their innocence and wonder has been an immeasurable force on my journey.

Gabe, three, and Zach, one

Zach, three and Gabe, five

The accumulation of *guk* in childhood is, unfortunately, relatively common. The difference between children taking experiences in stride or having those experiences result in longer-lasting negativity often depends on whether an adult is overseeing their interpretation of the world. Take an unfortunate yet innocent event that occurred to a friend of mine. When her son was about four, he walked in on his mother and father in bed. And no, they weren't sleeping. Yes, they stopped when they saw him. Weeks later they noticed that their son was avoiding his father. When they asked the child why, he wouldn't talk. Not connecting the two events, they took the boy to a therapist. Eventually the boy told the therapist he was scared of his father because he saw him hurt his mother. Once identified, the problem could be resolved. Had the parents not sought help, however, this one incident might have severely harmed the relationship between the father and son. That's why I like to remind parents: *you can't protect your children from everything that occurs in life, but what you can do is look for signs of unhealthiness and help them understand what they are experiencing in language appropriate for their developmental age.* What this means is, parents don't have to be perfect. Humans aren't meant to be perfect. Healthy adults are, however, accountable for their responsibilities, including the endless and sometimes thankless honor of parenting. And from this accountability come healthy, authentic adults.

Defense mechanisms and resiliency are interrelated factors that affect our ability to feel peace with who we are. The insight derived from understanding these protective factors not only allows you to discover more of your puzzle pieces, but also challenges you to advocate an important message for future generations: that genuine humanness can best be reached by diminishing the need for such protection.

CHAPTER EIGHT

Trail Notes

- ⋃ Defense mechanisms are meant as short-term aids

- ⋃ The more resilience one has and the less need for resilience one has, the better

- ⋃ Negative triggers are clues to unhealthiness

- ⋃ How parents respond to unhealthiness is what often prevents or creates guk

- ⋃ Through understanding ourselves, we can benefit future generations

Chapter Nine

Growing Up is Hard to Do, the Sequel

Individuation and the Familial Plight

Our first apartment sat next to a park, allowing Gabe and Zach, at one and three, to enjoy the simple things in our state of poverty. Gliding down the slide, catching bugs, and climbing just about anything that stood still long enough to let them on board became routine outlets for their unending toddler energy. Watching their interactions caused me to question what I was like at that age, and my curiosity grew as I attempted to understand the minds of these little humans. Each day my amazement at their accomplishments grew and, by the end of each developmental stage, I was easily convinced that it was my favorite and that I didn't want it to end. Never before had I been so utterly fascinated with anything except, of course, horses.

Without a car, our life revolved around the city bus schedule. Schlepping through the rain with a stroller, backpack, diaper bag, purse,

Gabe, four, and Zach, two

and umbrella while carrying Zach and holding on to Gabe's hand, a thirty-minute grocery store run could easily turn into hours. Adding to the stress of my ordeal were my fellow bus riders who readily expressed their displeasure. "Hurry up and get your kids on the bus. You're making us late." Many times near tears, I kept my thoughts to myself, trying to save the little energy I had for the bigger events yet to come, such as the actual grocery shopping. No matter how I tried, I could not find a way to carry more than one bag of groceries back to our apartment via the bus with two toddlers and our accompanying baggage. As my frustration at this grew, my fall from grace materialized to what may have been an illegal act: pushing a grocery cart home. With Zach in the front of the cart cushioned by his diaper bag and my purse, and Gabe squished in the back surrounded by groceries, I finally was able to buy enough food for more than a couple of days. The embarrassment of becoming the neighborhood *bag lady* was a price I was willing to pay.

While once able to maintain my privacy quite easily, Gabe and Zach's whitish-blond hair and contagious smiles possessed a knack for generating unsolicited attention. Such was the day the cashier looked at Gabe and remarked, "My, you have a pretty sister." While I responded with a simple smile due to my embarrassment over not cutting Zach's hair any time recently, Gabe initiated a more matter-of-fact approach, unequivocally blurting out, "That's not my sister. He has a penis!" Such was the first of many more incidents that breached my solitude.

CHAPTER NINE

College challenged my isolative tendencies as well, and I forced myself to become more assertive by taking communication classes, a subject that later became my major. Determined to overcome my deficits, my propensity for over-achieving took hold and I dismissed anything less than an "A" as *not good enough*, especially as I competed for scholarships and a place at the university. In my mind, my goals were simple and clear-cut: to take care of my children and graduate from college – at the top of my class, of course.

At Christmas time we walked to the nearest tree stand and, without a car, dragged the tree home. To keep costs down, we decorated it with paper cutouts and popcorn strings. We also began our tradition of eating Chinese food on Christmas Eve, if for no other reason than the only restaurant within walking distance was the Oriental one on the corner. I saved money by using cloth diapers and, at a rather low point, selling my beloved European English saddle. At the time, the possibility of ever owning a horse again seemed bleak. I sold other items over the years as well, though nothing of equal monetary or sentimental value.

Not long after we moved out, Tess and her family left Oregon for her husband's new job in Texas. Though certainly an unfair trade, I inherited their old blue Chevy Bobcat complete with a leaky roof and permanently closed driver's side door. Yes, a dream come true. Having a car changed my life. No longer did I need to rely on the bus or borrow grocery carts. But more than that, the added freedom renewed my dwindling hope.

Although striving to look at life optimistically, Tess's absence spawned familiar feelings of loneliness, and potential friendships from school proved short-lived due to my moodiness and rigid schedule. Consumed by life from dawn to near midnight, my routine didn't allow for socialization or complications. When problems did arise, my lack of skills to resolve them became evident through frustration and tears. Day to day I worried about how I was going to pay the bills, if I had enough money for food, and what would happen if I wasn't able to complete college. Adding to my internal conflict was the knowledge that my mother lived less than an hour away but never offered any support. I might have understood her absence had she not continually preached the importance of family being there for one another, but in my state of need, the emptiness of her words resulted in only anger and confusion. Lacking the courage to confront the issue due to believing I would somehow end up to blame, I reverted to what I knew best: avoidance. I could no longer support the hollow notion that *everything was fine*. A turning point of sorts, I chose to put my children first, knowing I lacked the energy and mental capacity to keep both her and my sons happy. Yet, as a daughter still looking for acceptance from her mother, I felt as though I was trapped in quicksand, doomed no matter what my action or inaction.

Living next door to my landlords proved both a blessing and a curse. While the wife loved Gabe and Zach and sometimes kept me company, the husband did not tolerate noise and demonstrated his agitation by yelling and banging on our adjoining cardboard-like wall, especially at night when I was attempting to wean Zach. Too timid to say anything to him, I finally gave in, and Zach remained on the bottle far beyond the advice of baby experts. Some things, I discovered, needed compromising. I could not be perfect, a realization I fought and fought and fought. In the end, I learned to pick my battles, though I resented it immensely.

After two years at the community college, I graduated number one in my class, an honor that came with giving the commencement address. As I wrote the speech, my depression reached a new low and by graduation night it took every ounce of effort I had in order to stand in front of hundreds of faces and give a speech I knew was less than what I was capable of writing. Long and drawn out, I not only mispronounced a word, but also nearly had to quit after my mouth became so

CHAPTER NINE

dry I had difficulty speaking. Only the thought of Gabe and Zach saw me through to the end, an inner voice demanding *you have to do this!* Although I received my high school diploma, my associate's degree, two awards for achievement, and three scholarships, not one person in the audience was cheering for me in particular. On a night that should have been spent celebrating with family and friends, I wondered how I had reached a place of such internal and external seclusion.

The author giving her commencement speech

As the mother of two grown sons, I believe my greatest accomplishment in life is over. Yes, a strong statement. I cannot imagine anything surpassing the privilege of guiding once dependent beings to that of healthy independent adults. Even if I was awarded a Nobel Peace Prize or, yes, won a gold medal at the Olympics in Grand Prix horse jumping, I still believe mothering would reach a place in my heart untouchable by other accolades.

This realization came to me as I prepared for my oldest son's wedding. Throughout the process of helping him and his bride plan the event, I found myself reminiscing over his life. Gabe and I had always been close, similar in many respects. Besides introverts and morning people, we are both also analytical, sensitive, animal lovers, dreamers, and driven. Growing up, he was a constant helper – my *guk* guy. Now, I felt a shift in our relationship. And as much as I preach to parents about anticipating their child's next developmental stage, I failed to do this in my own life. Oh, intellectually I considered it, but I hadn't really thought about how his getting married would affect me emotionally. Then, all of a sudden, I felt this wave of grief come over me one day, coupled with a reluctance to let go. Even though I realized this desire for him to be dependent on me again insulted every piece of knowledge I valued, the feeling would not go away. He had been *mine* for twenty-five years, after all, and I wanted things to stay the same. I cherished *the good old days* and I began daydreaming about how I wished he were still fifteen, or better yet, five. Yes, five, my perpetual kindergartener. If only I could have stopped the clock. But just as I was deep in my fantasy, the voice of reality knocked me in the head: "That's not a parent's job."

"But, but, but… it's so unfair!" the voice in my head defended.

"Ah… fairness," soothed my somewhat sarcastic alter ego. "Fairness has so little to do with parenting."

Not until I began choosing a song for our mother-son dance did I absorb the truth of that statement. In order to allow my son to move on healthily to the next phase of *his* life, I needed to move on to the next phase of *my* life, whether I wanted to or not. Tepidly, I looked for lyrics that symbolized this transition in both our lives. After listening to what seemed like every trite, gushy, silly, stupid, sappy, corny, syrupy song ever written for a mother and son – and let me tell you, there are a lot of them – I heard *it. The* perfect song: *Watching You Go* by MotherLode Trio. Tears flowed even before the prelude began, all some seventy-six times. So beautifully the words define the bittersweet job of a parent having to let go of a child. Countless boxes of tissues later, I claimed to be ready to dance to a tune that equated the piercing of my heart with a spear. The time had come for me to both celebrate *and* grieve my son's departure from me, the ultimate polar conflict for a parent. Moments like these have a way of illuminating the inevitable: if you want to maintain emotional balance and healthy relationships, *ya gotta keep up*. Life is harsh that way.

🥾 *Exercise 9a: If you had to summarize your current relationship with your parent(s), what would you say? Write your answer to this question on your timeline.*

A parent-child relationship is a dance of delicate balance. Beginning as one and separating into two beings, a mother begins letting go at birth, deciding each day how much control to maintain and how much freedom to provide. For eighteen years, a parent must progressively teach all life's lessons at each developmental stage so increased independence is achieved, all the while remaining the steady base of safety, support, encouragement, nurturance, and education. When this occurs healthily, the child gradually learns what is necessary in order to attain and sustain individual health and preparedness for life. Simply, childhood is the place to acquire the tools needed for adulthood.

Watching You Go touches on what Swiss psychiatrist Carl Jung referred to as *individuation,* a process wherein children separate from their parents in order to find their own identity while simultaneously maintaining a healthy connectedness to their family of origin. Sounds easy, right? Well, I'll let you decide for yourself.

While many cultures have *rights of passage* ceremonies in order to complete and celebrate this pathway to adulthood, our society tends to lack such rituals. Some tribes in Africa, for example, separate young boys from their families and teach them about their heritage, cultural legends, skills, and leadership in preparation for adulthood. Likewise, in *Long Road to Freedom*, Nelson Mandela talks about the transition from boy to manhood in his tribe through circumcising the adolescent boys, the cut historically symbolizing the shedding of a snake's skin fortifying a rebirth to manhood. Somewhere along the way, I think that sentiment was lost when the procedure made its way to the United States. These coming-of-age rituals communicate and celebrate the new responsibilities expected in adulthood and take place with great pride and respect under the supervisory and supportive eye of the community, especially the elders whose wisdom is revered. In the United States, aside from a few cultural-specific celebrations or one's eighteenth birthday, the majority of young people enter adulthood with little hoopla or clear expectation as to what the whole of this transition to adulthood represents. And this is problematic.

Without rituals and societal unity, the responsibility of ensuring healthy individuation defaults to parents. Though some parents do a tremendous job of preparing their children for adulthood, as a societal whole we are less triumphant. We may have high expectations of our new, young adults, but the path to successful individuation often remains obscure. In terms of horse jumping, it is comparable to enthusiastically signing up for an eight-jump hunt course and expecting to win without bothering to look at the route or design. Unless great luck is on your side, the result would probably not be that pretty. Most serious competitors first walk a jumping course, taking into account the length of their horse's stride, the height of the jumps, and the distances between the jumps. Have I mentioned that knowledge is priceless? So too is preparation or, as I often call it: prevention. Successful individuation takes understanding, planning, and implementation.

CHAPTER NINE

🌵 *Exercise 9b: Consider how you prepared for adulthood. Did your parents talk to you about what it meant to become an adult? What lessons were presented to you? Did you know what was expected of you as you turned eighteen? Did you attend any type of ritual? Did you consider turning eighteen as an event that added responsibility to your life? Write your thoughts on your timeline.*

Imagine buying a car only to have it crash into a fence because the manufacturer forgot the step on the assembly line where they install the brakes. Children are similarly vulnerable. During the eighteen years our society gives parents to raise a child, there are certain topics that need addressed so that individuation is victorious. I call them *The Nine Necessities*. Each topic summarizes an area for discussion during each developmental stage until a competent understanding of healthiness transpires. This concept differs little from learning how to read, with each grade level allowing for advancement in both knowledge and skill. The following is a short description of each category:

1) Physical and Emotional Self-Care: *insight into holistic healthiness*
2) Finances: *responsible money management*
3) Relationships: *the consideration of boundaries, support, and self-respect*
4) Communication: *disciplining oneself to be honest, respectful, and direct with purpose*
5) Partnerships: *understanding love, sex, infatuation, lust, intimacy, co-habitation, marriage, and commitment*
6) Problem Solving: *the art of creative thinking and considering consequences*
7) Education and Knowledge: *the value of information, making mistakes, and continued learning*

8) Accountability, Responsibility, Ethics, and Morals: *using integrity as the foundation for individual and societal functioning*
9) Life Skills, Purpose, and Pleasure: *appreciating the importance of minimizing stress, finding meaning, and giving back to society*

The reality of why many children find themselves unprepared for adulthood hit me one night when I was teaching a parenting class for moms and dads of pre-schoolers. One of my favorite questions to ask parents is this: "At what age do you think parenting gets easier?" Undoubtedly, many parents answer, "Around ten or twelve." When I ask why that particular age, they respond with something like, "Because children are able to do things on their own." While it is true children become more independent around that age, what parents sometimes fail to take into account are the invisible needs that increase at the same time. Ignoring a dirty diaper or a screaming four year old is often hard to do, but the silent cues of a pre-teenager needing guidance are much more subtle. Although children have emotional needs at all ages, around upper grade school there is a type of role-reversal that can go unnoticed if parents aren't paying attention. Instead of demanding parents' time, children wait for the parents to intervene. This becomes problematic when parents interpret the silence as the child having less or no parental needs, as was the consensus of most of the parents in my class. I look at it this way: while children under the age of ten might require more attention for their physical needs, children over ten require more uninvited involvement for their emotional needs.

Exercise 9c: Out of 'The Nine Necessities', write the ones on your timeline that you think you needed more education about in preparing for adulthood. How did the absence of this knowledge affect you as an adult? Have you since attempted to gain information on the topic?

Reality would prove that most of us entered adulthood absent of some of the wisdom of *The Nine Necessities*. If nothing else, this list validates parenting as a vital, all-encompassing, immeasurable job where gaps are bound to occur. Once you become aware of your voids as an adult, you have two options. One, you can choose to acquire the needed information or, two, you can choose to let the voids in your life prevent you from reaching your potential. Consider this: if you feel stuck in life, or as if something is missing or isn't working, perhaps you are simply lacking some knowledge you failed to gain in childhood. When I feel this way, the words of English novelist George Eliot inspire me to seek out what I need: "It's never too late to be who you might have been."

Exercise 9d: In exercise 4a you listed the roadblocks that stood in the way of five of your life's goals. Now consider in which of 'The Nine Necessities' categories each roadblock belongs and add it to your timeline.

While traditional individuation looks at a child's ability to transition to adulthood, I believe this is only half the story. Successful individuation also speaks to a parent's ability to healthily separate from the child. Unless a parent prepares and supports a child during individuation and is ready to endure healthy yet painful growth, individuation will most certainly fall short for the child or, at the least, become a much more difficult process.

MotherLode Trio sums up parenting well:

> *It's true what they say about all this – indeed you changed my life.*
> *How could so much sacrifice bring one so much joy.*
> *But from that first hello I've been practicing my goodbyes, my goodbyes.*
> *I watched you crawl, I watched you sleep, I watched you fall, I watched you need me.*
> *It's so bittersweet watching you go.*

When an eighteen year old leaves home, and yes, I'm begging optimism here, the parent-child relationship must change in order to remain healthy. But for many parents – a category in which I include myself – it's difficult to turn *off* the parent button. The deceiving aspect about parenthood when you are at the hospital euphorically cooing over miniature toes and fingers is that you fail to consider the job description ever changing. In order for children to reach adulthood prepared for independence, however, parents must be willing to weave through an emotional and diverse course.

The author dancing with Gabe at his wedding

From the parental perspective, successful individuation means that *equal adult* replaces the title of legal guardian. Likewise, as children individuate to adulthood, one of the transformations necessary is to view one's parents as individuals rather than authoritarians, acknowledging that asking permission is no longer required. This, of course, is made much easier if parents rescind the parental influence that makes their children feel inferior or dutiful. I even had one teenager who used her mother's words against her by putting a spin on a common parental phrase. "When you treat me like an adult, I'll act like one!" I have to admit I had to chuckle at the truth behind her statement.

Exercise 9e: When you make a decision, do you ever feel you need your parents' permission? Are you ever afraid to tell your parents something because you fear their response? When do you feel empowered in your relationship with your parents? When do you feel uncomfortable in your relationship with your parents? When you are with your parents, do you act like an adult or do you revert to child-like behaviors? Do you ever feel as though your parents still have child-like expectations of you? If your parents are deceased, these questions can still be helpful. Just because our parents may not be living does not mean they cease to have power over us.

As adulthood approaches for a child, it is healthy for the parent-child relationship to take on new boundaries expected of an equal union. Sometimes in therapy I'll ask a mother and her adult child to pretend they just met in order to make a point. Starting with a clean slate allows them to think about how they would define their relationship as adults. Pretending to have no history together, we then look at the *guk* that gets in the way of them maintaining healthy roles. This process does not occur overnight, of course, and takes a conscious effort by both parties in order to grieve aspects of the past that are gone as well as change behavior that is no longer advantageous to the new adult relationship. I find resolving individuation issues to be one of the most beneficial when working toward personal wholeness because the process often helps to pinpoint unhealthiness that keeps a person stuck in childhood. Successful individuation realigns the power in a parent-child relationship and ultimately gives the child permission to mature into adulthood.

Exercise 9f: Have you defined any past unhealthiness pertaining to your parents? If "yes", has the issue(s) been resolved? If not, what is the roadblock? Summarize your thoughts on your timeline.

In chapter three I asked you to write a job description for parents. The reason this question is important is because it is now time to think about the flip side.

🥾 *Exercise 9g: If you wrote a job description for children, what would it say? Add this to your timeline.*

Earlier I defined a parent's job as *preparing one's child to become an independent, emotionally healthy, well-adjusted, socially conscious, responsible, productive adult.* If you remember, I also stated my short version: *to nurture, educate, and support a child toward authenticity.* Now I will tell you my job description for a child: *to strive to become an authentic adult.* This, of course, constitutes becoming an independent, emotionally healthy, well-adjusted, socially conscious, responsible, productive adult. Make sense? Consider this: if my job is to teach you to ride a horse, then your job is to learn how to ride the horse. If we didn't know our individual roles, the result would most likely suffer. Disappointing outcomes occur when parents fail to define and maintain healthy roles. And this brings us to another question that is now important to consider.

🥾 *Exercise 9h: What, if anything, do you think children owe their parents? Write your answer on your timeline.*

One of the greatest sacrifices I see as a therapist stems from adults who continue down a particular road in life because they are still trying to win their parents' love or make their parents proud of them. Sadly, these individuals often have little insight as to the destruction they are causing their inner spirits. While it is human nature to want to be loved and accepted by one's parents, the failure to understand, grieve, and problem solve this as a loss when it doesn't materialize can leave adults vulnerable to persecuting emptiness. These individuals are essentially stuck in a child-like phase of development because they think happiness will only result when their parents fulfill this need. Worse yet, these individuals commonly feel responsible for this failure and endure an undying obligation to try to correct what is often an uncompromising situation. This psychological injustice is what perpetuates my crusade for both self-awareness and parental education, and founds my beliefs regarding a child's role in the family. There is no doubt in my mind that self-acceptance is achieved more easily through the venue of healthy parenting, and that healthy parenting is a societal goal worth prioritizing.

I am a firm believer in one-sided obligation for healthy parent-child relationships. Parents choose to *oblige* the needs of the child they bring into this world. For clarity, oblige means *to bind somebody morally or legally to do something*. The child, on the other hand, does not have *obligations*. The child has *needs*. The fulfillment of these needs is a parent's obligation. To allocate, profess, or insinuate indebtedness upon a child is problematic. Unhealthiness occurs when parents expect their children to be anything other than children learning to become authentic adults. This means that treating a child as a friend, caretaker, servant, confidant, or as property takes away from the designated role of the child. Parents who require their children to pursue certain occupations, maintain specific beliefs, or live a particular lifestyle interfere with their ability to discover wholeness. In my experience, many parents compel these unhealthy mandates under the umbrella of *loyalty, duty,* and *respect*. Underneath this umbrella is the parental belief that their children *owe* them. The irony in this belief is that the *respect* so many parents attempt to demand from their children usually materializes automatically when parents meet their children's needs unconditionally. Moreover, the only thing healthy parents *want* from their children is the satisfaction of knowing that they become whole, healthy adults.

Trail Notes

- Healthy individuation founds a child's adult life

- Parents have an obligation to their children; children have needs for their parents to fulfill

- A child's job is to learn how to become authentic

- *The Nine Necessities* define areas where childhood voids may have originated

- It is never too late to become who you want to be

Chapter Ten

I Left My Heart in Days Gone By

Grief and the Discovery of Loss

Due to our divorce, trips to California defined summers for Gabe and Zach so they could spend time with their father. Sometimes I would drive them, sometimes they would fly, and once we took the train. Wanting them to have positive childhood memories, I often forfeited practicality. If I waited until I could afford it, I rationalized, it would never happen. The topic of internal debate at the time was whether to rent a convertible and drive Gabe and Zach to their dad's home. In this particular scenario, conservatism lost. I chose adventure.

Despite understanding the importance for each of my sons to develop a strong relationship with their father, having them gone for two months selfishly tore at my heart. Without their visibility, I had only a self-promise to prevent me from screwing up this nebulous thing called *parenting*. From day to day, my internal demons distracted my focus and motivation, leaving me feeling lost. As if a puppet controlled by strings, I felt powerless over my body and began to wonder if I would ever be free from these emotional fiends.

I found some reprieve by distracting myself with summer school and putting together care packages for Gabe and Zach. Counting down the days to their return, I cleaned their room, bought their school supplies, and if I had enough money, placed a few new toys in their room. Nothing gave me more pleasure than seeing the unassuming delight in their eyes when I surprised them. This practice grew throughout their childhoods, from toys to birthday parties to trips to, one time, a puppy. Probably because of my childhood experiences, I had not envisioned the extent of joy my sons would add to my life. Brian had been the one who felt comfortable around children, not me. The moment I fell in love with Brian was from my lounge chair as I watched him play with all the children in a pool while vacationing. Children naturally gravitated toward him, and I daydreamed about the large, fun-loving family we would have one day. When Gabe was born, I felt my dream coming true. I even remember half-jokingly asking Brian on the way home from the hospital, "Well, are you ready to have another son?" Twenty months later, not even having picked out a girl's name, my wish materialized with Zachary. Now, each summer, the grief stemming from that broken dream materialized through an empty house, knowing that my children were over 800 miles away and that their father would never be coming home.

My sophomore year at the university began with decreased expectations of myself. With my depression equating the likes of trudging through mud in steel boots, I realized that maintaining a high grade-point average lacked feasibility. Overshadowed by the looming fear of how I was going to provide for my children once I graduated, I grew to care less about learning and more about my ability to obtain employment. Reminiscent of my feelings during high school, I wondered why I was trying to do *normal* things when I obviously lacked normalcy. I convinced myself that even my choice of major confirmed my doomed future, and I kept wondering what possessed me to pursue a degree in speech communications when I dreaded talking.

One of the upsides of attending college was having time to volunteer in Gabe and Zach's classrooms. Few things gave me more pleasure than participating and sharing in their day. Learning about the needs of children, these experiences resulted in two new family rituals: *Friday family night* and *alone time*. On *Friday family night* we made our favorite tacos and chocolate cokes and chose a movie to watch together that had a positive message for us to discuss. *Alone time* was a period I scheduled each week with the boys separately in order to grow and develop our individual relationships. One of these events sparked Zach's curiosity and he soon asked, "Mom, what do you do all day?" With that, I decided to take each of them to my college classes with me. Zach's visit coincided with a communications class in which we were reading fairytales using different voices for each character. At three years old, I think the stories mesmerized him as much as he did the female students in the class with his long eyelashes, cherry plump cheeks, and infectious smile. During Gabe's visit, instead of practicing his alphabet as we had planned, he listened to the lecture and raised his hand when the professor asked if there were any questions. Rather advanced for his five years, it's possible Gabe and I shared about the same academic ability. The difference was, he impressed my professor.

Early in my senior year, I began experiencing a deep pain in my lower abdomen followed by a tightening in my upper body and arms, causing numbing in my extremities, and making breathing difficult. The first time this occurred, I thought I might be having a heart attack. Unable to focus, I pulled my car over and took a deep breath, slowly letting it out until the pain subsided. When the episode was over, I downplayed it as a sole event, convincing myself it was nothing. When the symptoms reoccurred with heightened intensity and uncontrollable crying, I felt forced to seek help. Not knowing where to turn, I wound up in an emergency room. When the doctor asked what was wrong, I embarrassingly spewed between sobs, "I can't stop crying." Without comment, the doctor walked out of the room and, a few moments later, a man walked in. "You're in the wrong place," he declared. And with that, he escorted me to the exit. Shy and obedient and not fully registering what had just occurred, I concluded it to be validation that I was not only crazy, but also that there was no help for me. Years later, I realized the experience had been my first exposure to the stigma surrounding mental health, though it would not be my last.

I don't remember how I found out about the counseling center at the university, but in the midst of one of my despairing moments, I called and made an appointment. By the time I found the correct old brick building in the midst of many lookalikes, my composure had crumbled. Hearing my name called, I sheepishly walked into the therapist's office desperately trying to hold in my tears. Distrusting everything about the scenario, I positioned myself carefully in case I needed to bolt toward freedom. Then, just when I needed something to make me want to stay, I heard, "I'm glad you came in today." Months later, I measured my progress in therapy by my ability to formulate three words I had never spoken aloud before: *My father drank*.

At semester's end, my therapist left the university to open a private practice. With little desire to find someone new, I convinced myself I was fine. In my defense, I did not consider my depressed mood a symptom. My reserved, sad, moody, low-energy existence was all I knew. It was my *normal*.

As I neared graduation, my part-time employer informed me that the company was moving to Arizona and asked if we were interested in relocating with them. After discussing the pros and cons with Gabe and Zach, the decision was unanimous. We were leaving the cold and rain of Oregon for sunny Arizona. Two weeks before moving, I graduated with my Bachelor's Degree in Speech Communications, though I was far from the top of my class.

"When we are wounded by loss, what we bleed is grief." The words of grief specialist Steven C. Kalas stunned me the first time I heard them. In the midst of therapeutic enlightenment, I was beginning to acknowledge the parade of voids in my life as being not only significant losses, but also worthy of my grieving. Not unlike death, each loss had left emptiness within me unfilled by something I longed for in my life. Still, the idea my childhood voids were due to circumstances out of my control defied what I had grown up believing: that *I* was to blame – that *I* became suicidal because I was a hideous person who didn't deserve to live.

Loss is a human reality. No matter if you define your childhood as healthy, dysfunctional, or abusive, I guarantee you experienced some type of loss. Whether or not you have acknowledged your past losses is a different question. For whatever reason, and I imagine it has to do with us humans not recognizing the value of our feelings, loss is something we like to ignore or downplay. Given that you are on a trail of self-exploration, however, loss is no doubt one of the obstacles you will stumble upon and need to know how to respond to fittingly.

🥾. *Exercise 10a: Think about any losses you remember from your childhood and write them on your timeline at the age they occurred.*

As you begin to identify your losses, you will probably realize the diversity of losses a person can experience in childhood. I have divided them into five categories with examples. Keep in mind some of these categories overlap. They are:

1) A Physical Loss: *death or absence of a person or animal, virginity, possession, home*
2) A Need: *shelter, food, trust, attachment, safety, or belonging*
3) An Experience: *prom, sport, mother-daughter tea*
4) A Life Skill: *any of 'The Nine Necessities'*
5) An Expectation, Hope, or Dream: *having two parents who live together, a parent coming to a school event or sport, a birthday party, owning a pet*

Important point: *Every person defines his or her own losses.* Consider two individuals who lose their jobs. Individual A responds happily because he found the job boring and low in pay. Individual B, however, is sad because he thought the job was challenging, fulfilling, and paid well. Only one of these individuals will grieve the loss of his job. On the other hand, the spouses of individual A and B might feel differently because each is looking at the job loss from their own perspective. Maybe the spouse of individual B is happy about the job loss because the hours were long and interfered with family life. As with other aspects of self-discovery, defining your losses is a personal exploration and will be most valuable to you if founded by your deepest truth and not someone else's opinion or society's expectation.

When looking back at your childhood, finding the source of a loss is helpful because it can affect your emotional response. Imagine growing up without a father because he abandoned your family. Now imagine growing up without a father because a drunk driver killed him. If you're anything like I am, different emotions surface depending on the reason for the father's absence. Your response to a loss is an important piece to your puzzle because this may affect how you problem-solve the void caused by the loss, a topic covered in the next chapter. Questioning the *why* behind your losses is one of the factors to keep in mind as we proceed.

 Exercise 10b: Now that we have defined different types of losses, think back over your childhood and add any other losses you remember. Then next to each loss, write down what type of loss it represents (physical, need, experience, life skill, or expectation, hope, or dream). As you continue your trail ride, add additional losses and type as you identify them.

The next step on your journey is to assess each loss in your life as either *primary* or *secondary*. I like to look at it this way: *primary* losses are what begin the sequence of events that later found *secondary* losses. If your boss fired you and the bank repossessed your car because you failed to make the payment, for example, the *primary loss* is losing your job and the *secondary loss* is losing your car. In other words, it would be logical to conclude that had you not lost your job, you would have made your car payment.

While the example of losing your job and car are concrete physical losses, many of the losses we incur in childhood are emotional or developmental and can be more difficult to identify. My outings with my father, for example, created numerous losses for me, including the loss of feeling cared about and the loss of feeling safe. Over time, these losses helped create a rippling affect for more losses to occur, such as the loss of self-esteem, confidence, and trust.

Before I move on, I need to clarify a sometimes-confusing topic. What I am describing is a *correlation* between two events, not *cause and effect*. Cause and effect is a term used when "if A occurs, then B occurs" every time. If you turn a glass of water upside down, for example, the water will spill out every time unless gravity magically disappears at that same moment. In the discoveries you are making, whether or not B occurs after A, and to what extent, is dependent upon numerous factors, including one's temperament, personality, and environment, with each experience being unique.

When parents bring their children to me for therapy, the presenting problem is often a symptom of a prior problem, or *a secondary loss*. *Acting out* behaviors are most often secondary losses. My pulling Travis's hair, skipping school, poor grades, disrespectful behavior, and use of alcohol could all be traced back to other issues. This makes finding the primary loss an important part of my job as a therapist. If I were to focus only on eliminating the visible unwanted behavior, another unwanted behavior would most likely develop due to the primary loss – the source of the child's pain – remaining unresolved.

Primary losses remain unresolved in childhood for numerous reasons. In some cases parents deny or minimize the existence of a problem. Other times there is a lack of knowledge as to the impact caused by a particular incident (ignorance). Too often, nobody wants to upset the status quo. In my family, I think all these factors played a part. Had someone confronted my secondary losses, the result may have exposed the secret of my father's alcoholism. I experienced many cases as a crisis counselor where the parents' dysfunction was at the root of the child's crisis. The parents, however, usually deflected focus to the child, stating, "Oh, he never listens" or "She's just a bad kid". Seldom did the parents look for the cause of the crisis, see the crisis as an escalation of other events, or believe they had a part in the unwanted behavior. This lack of awareness made much of my job about education. Far too common is for children to become scapegoats solely because their behavior is the most visible. It is easier to point to the child and place blame rather than reveal ignorance, dysfunction, or abuse within a family. In their powerless role, children are easy targets. The bottom line is this: detecting un-health is the best deterrent to secondary losses.

Unless the primary loss is rectified, unhealthy consequences will no doubt continue. This is why your behavior is an important aspect along your trail ride to understand.

Exercise 10c: On your timeline, label each of your losses as primary or secondary. Now look for any correlations between your acting out behaviors, your personality characteristics, your defense mechanisms, and any childhood invasions. Where do any concerning areas fall in relation to the theories of Maslow and Erikson? Questioning associations is helpful. When I look at my early teenage years on my timeline and see that I overdosed on pain pills, for example, I ask "Why?" When I answer, "Because I felt lonely and hopeless," I again ask "Why?" This eventually leads me to my feeling unloved by my father, which is shown on my timeline by some of my early experiences with him. Discovering primary losses is a process. Keep in mind we feel and behave certain ways for particular reasons and those reasons are important to understand so resolution can occur.

At this point you probably recognize how the information in the prior nine chapters interrelates. By understanding healthy from normal, the purpose of emotions, the difference between healthy and unhealthy, acting out, attachment and development, personality and temperament, defense mechanisms, resiliency, and the process of individuation, you now have the basis for identifying the truths of your childhood story. When you look at your timeline, you should see a picture developing, allowing you to view the progression of how you developed into the person you are today. By identifying the healthy and unhealthy aspects of your life, you can then determine which of your puzzle pieces are missing, damaged, or misplaced.

As you identify the losses in your life, you will no doubt find situations that you have yet to grieve, have not grieved completely, or that you may not be ready to grieve. I like the saying, *You are where you are.* I don't believe the process of self-actualization can be hurried. Nor do I believe grieving has a timeline. Grief is a personal experience wherein no two people grieve the same way. In other words, there is no *right* or *wrong* way to grieve. The only common denominator worthy of mentioning is that healthy grieving facilitates healing and the ability to move forward. When you begin to grieve your losses, try to understand what you are feeling and allow any emotions to surface non-judged. Remember, emotions have a purpose. Interpret their messages, not your opinions of them.

Exercise 10d: How did you learn about grieving? How did each of your parents grieve? Looking at each of the losses on your timeline, write down the way(s) in which you responded to each loss. Circle each loss you feel you are still grieving.

Earlier I talked about how triggers help define your *guk*. Consider that the total of who you are equates to a certain amount of energy. For easy measure, let's pretend your *guk* bag is half full. This means you have only fifty percent of your energy left to engage in the present day and the planning of your future. Living with this energy-zapping *guk* is similar to being in debt and having to spend your paycheck on credit card bills instead of what you want. This, in turn, creates more *guk* because debt causes more stress. Only when you take action to identify and resolve your financial issues can you change the outcome. *Guk* is the same way. By resolving problems from the past and freeing up this wasted energy, you give yourself more power and control over your present-day and future life.

By understanding the losses in your past, you are then able to take the next step: identifying the void that the loss may have produced. Losing a loved one, for instance, can result in the void of a friendship, intimacy, a tennis partner, or income. A less direct example is my dropping out of high school. This loss created an educational void, but also a void of belonging to a particular group. Another way to look at voids is to consider what didn't materialize because of the loss. I often wonder, for example, what going to my high school prom might have been like. Missing this high school ritual caused me to not only feel a void of normalcy and belonging, but also the void of identifying with my high school class and subsequent class reunions. These voids made up some of the missing, damaged, and misplaced pieces to my puzzle. You will find your puzzle pieces, as well, through the truthful exploration of your childhood.

Besides allowing us to grieve, the other purpose behind understanding our losses is so we have the opportunity to fill the missing entity, if needed. The following are categories that define the different type of voids a loss might create:

1) a skill,
2) an event,
3) a developmental stage,
4) a relationship, and
5) knowledge.

In the next chapter we will discuss different ways to satisfy voids. Right now, what is most important is to identify your losses and the voids they represent.

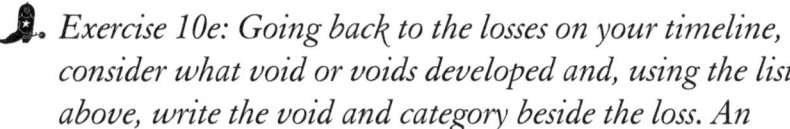 *Exercise 10e: Going back to the losses on your timeline, consider what void or voids developed and, using the list above, write the void and category beside the loss. An*

example in my life was the loss of a responsible father figure (a need), and this resulted in voids in all the categories, though a few examples are safety (developmental stage), feeling part of a family (relationship), having my father walk me down the aisle at my wedding (event), as well as knowledge and numerous skills one would expect a father to teach his child.

My grieving process officially began one afternoon as I sat at my kitchen table and heard a *thump* on one of the windows to the backyard. As I looked outside, I saw a bird lying on the ground, the victim of poor eyesight, I suspect, as I doubt my windows were clean. As I picked him up to nurse him back to health, I felt the warmth of his pulsating body come to an end. The realization he was dead initiated an insurmountable wave of sadness from the depth of my gut that pushed past my chest and exploded via a wail equivalent to that of a walrus cry. For the next exhausting thirty minutes my body involuntarily contracted and released noises unequal to any I had ever produced before, terminating only when I collapsed in a worn-out heap on the couch, sobs still dictating my movement. What I realized much later was that the little bird triggered all my unresolved losses by coming into my life when my body could not contain more energy. As if a volcano, the dead bird ignited my eruption of grief.

A few days later, I shared my story with my therapist, tentatively asking, "So…how long does this grieving thing take?"

"Grieving takes as long as it takes," he answered with a reassuring smile. Seeing that his words had not calmed me, he added, "And I've never had anyone tell me it wasn't worth the effort."

And to that I wholeheartedly agree.

Trail Notes

- Loss is inevitable; grieving takes as long as it takes and is a worthwhile venture

- Grieving past losses frees up energy for healthier pursuits

- Only you can define your losses

- Losses can be physical, needs, experiences, skills, expectations, hopes, or dreams

- Voids include skills, events, development, relationships, and knowledge

Chapter Eleven

Oops, I Messed Up Again
The Lost Art of Solving Problems

As our U-Haul crossed the Arizona border, a sense of déjà vu engulfed my body. Looking out onto the openness of the desert dotted with saguaros and other fascinating spiny creatures, the scene was reminiscent of my childhood fantasy of galloping across the sand against a soft warm wind, ignited perhaps by one too many episodes of *The Lone Ranger*. Intuitively, I knew I had found my home. Little did I realize how much I would come to identify with the desert through its outer toughness and inner hidden offerings.

Provided by my employer, our house resided in a resort-type setting with the family room acting as the business office. Gabe and Zach spent most of their time resembling frontiersmen as they explored the neighborhood, trekking through normally dry washes inhabited by wild cats, javelina, raccoons, scorpions, and snakes. Not surprisingly, a few of the critters made it to our doorstep with a pleading, "Can I keep him?" Most memorable was a particular cactus Gabe appraised worthy

Zach, four and Gabe, six

of capture, a decision he soon regretted when I had to pluck hundreds of minuscule cactus needles from his chest. Pleased with how our new life was falling into place, I delighted in seeing my children happy as much as I cherished the warmth of the sunshine. Unconvinced the sun would persist, however, I kept my shades open all night so the morning rays could awaken me, prompting me to walk outside to make sure there were no rain clouds lurking in the sky. Rarely was I disappointed.

One of the first people I met in Phoenix became a life-long friend and changed the course of my life. A businessman and philanthropist from Alaska, Sky attended one of the seminars where I worked, founding a unique yet mystical connection between us. Considering him the likes of a long-lost brother with a natural ease resonating our relationship, I found myself living vicariously though the stories of his entrepreneurial adventures and world travel. Over the following years as I descended emotionally and confronted the return of my anxiety attacks, he remained stable and supportive, allowing me a refreshing view of humanness. His respectfulness toward the boys and me cast doubt on my learned assumption that men were unreliable. Sky proved to be someone I could count on regardless of my depth of depression and propensity for bad decision-making.

Feeling a lack of purpose building in my life, I left my job the following year and we moved into a nearby apartment. My newly

CHAPTER ELEVEN

acquired independence sparked a longing for a dog for Gabe and Zach so they could experience the same kind of unconditional love I felt from Mike as I grew up. Thus began my search for a male, black Labrador puppy. Arriving at the address listed in an advertisement, I walked in the yard to find twenty-some puppies of various colors, shapes, and sizes. As I squatted down, the yippy, bouncy,

Swede as a puppy

furry balls of energy collectively found my lap and dug their needle-sharp teeth into my arms, apparently mistaking them for chew toys. While looking around for any black puppy, I noticed a blond Labrador mix sitting patiently beside me, her eyes longingly gazing at mine. And that was that. Swede, as we later named her, waited in our kitchen while I led my two blindfolded little boys into their surprise. As Swede quickly became the focal point of our lives, we took her on daily walks, to obedience class, and to sprinkler play dates during the warm Arizona evenings with her best friend, Norman, a boxer who lived nearby.

Norman and Swede playing

My new job introduced me to the field of mental health. Hired as an advocate for a five-year-old ward of the state, my duties entailed helping him stay on task at school and attending court proceedings relevant to his care. Brandon's story was one that would become familiar to me over the years. Abandoned by his drug-addicted parents, and with no relative able to serve as guardian, the State of Arizona placed him in a group home. Further victimized while at the group home, his acting out behaviors increased and he became ineligible for foster care or adoption.

Despite his troublesome behaviors, Brandon was difficult not to love. His precious smile and heartfelt desire to please easily melted my heart. Each morning when I arrived at his school, he was waiting at the playground gate with the eagerness of a canine eyeing his owner. Large for his age and emotionally vulnerable, Brandon was a target for bullies and these incidents left him confused and lonely. He attached easily to my presence and was steadfast in his requests to come live with me, a reality that made it even more difficult when my job lost its funding and I had to leave. Due to confidentiality laws, I was unable to contact Brandon, though I still often wonder about him. His gift to me was igniting my passion for children who have no voice with which to protect themselves, a field that would lure me back numerous times over the next couple of decades.

Feeling void of a foundation, a familiar urge to run began taunting me. I was frantic with indecision when Sky financed a house in which we could live, a gesture that influenced my life more than any other event past or since. Having a home to call my own gave me a sense of stability never before felt, dramatically reducing my worries. Deep in a cul-de-sac in a quiet neighborhood within walking distance to the boys' schools, the residence boasted a yard of nurtured green grass and automatic sprinklers for Swede, a bedroom for each of us, and a basketball hoop for Gabe and Zach. The boys' favorite part, however, was the beautiful brick fireplace in the living room where Santa made many highly anticipated arrivals. We lived in this home for nearly a decade, and our fond memories still endure.

filling the void more effective and less complicated. Let me give you an example. When I chose to work on my losses, I began with my dog, Mike, because I felt his death was at the core of my grief. Not having grieved his death when he died, I carried the sadness and guilt into adulthood with me. I regretted not being able to tell Mike that I loved him one last time, and I envisioned him scared and alone in a veterinarian's office when he died. Incidentally, one of the possible consequences when parents fail to discuss important events with their children is they will come up with their own view of what they think happened, whether accurate or not. I don't actually know the circumstances around Mike's death. As a child, however, I came to my own conclusion, and this conclusion resulted in my feeling angry and resentful. Although years later Max filled part of the void left by Mike's death, Max's death then caused the original loss to intensify because my loss included two dogs, each unique and requiring individualized grieving. In other words, getting another dog did not compensate for my need to grieve Mike. This is why both grieving *and* satisfying any void that materializes are two important but separate aspects of resolving your missing, damaged, or misplaced puzzle pieces. Simply filling a void without grieving the loss generally keeps *guk* stuck in your body.

When, as an adult, I decided to work through my grief, I planned a memorial service for Mike, and later did the same for Max. I made a cement headstone and decorated it with Mike's name and the sentiment *My Childhood Best Friend.* The stone now resides in an area of my yard designated for my deceased pets named *Swede's Garden of Love* in honor of Swede who died at the age of thirteen. During the process of making the stone, I was able to grieve Mike by reminiscing about his life and, when I laid the stone at its final resting place, I was able to tell him an official good-bye knowing, symbolically, that he was near me in spirit. Rituals such as memorial services, gravesites, and scattering ashes are all vehicles that promote the grieving process and help provide closure for losses. Losses other than death also benefit from these types of ceremonies. I have assisted people in putting hurtful memories to rest, burying lost dreams, and even celebrating the promise of the future by saying farewell to childhood *guk*.

Besides rituals, four other approaches can assist in grieving and lessening the voids produced by losses. Examples of each follow, along with the kind of loss and void as defined in the previous chapter.

Swede's Garden of Love

1) Ritual: A ceremony that honors a loss, as described above. My ritual for Mike signified a *physical* loss (death), and the void was a *relationship*.

2) Re-enactment: This reminds me of what Billy Crystal describes as a *do-over* or second chance in the movie, *City Slickers*. One of my do-overs was a formal dinner and dance I went to when I was in my thirties. This opportunity to get all gussied up and have a gorgeous man in a tuxedo pick me up and dance the night away was probably as close to a prom as I will ever get, and it served to lessen my grief and wonder about what such an experience would be like. This example signifies the loss of an *experience*, and the void was an *event*.

3) Replacement: Filling voids with what was lost is another option. I was able to compensate for not graduating high school by going to college and earning my high school diploma.

As I became aware of other deficits, such as communication, budgeting, and teamwork, I worked to fill those as well. Although I didn't grieve these voids in the same way as I did Mike, over time I felt a decrease in my frustration level as I became better skilled. Part of this relief came from not feeling as though I was playing *catch-up*. Up until then, the message in my head was, *I should already know how to do this.* This thought, in turn, caused me to question my *what ifs*, such as: *What if I had grown up healthily? Would I be further along in my career? Would I be a better parent? Would I still be married?* Prior to replacing my voids, questions such as these kept me stuck in a perpetual cycle of feeling inadequate and flawed. These losses represented *life skills, expectations, and dreams.* The associated voids included *skills, knowledge, relationships,* and *events.* As mentioned previously, sometimes losses overlap into more than one category and sometimes losses incur multiple voids.

4) Surrogacy: Sometimes losses result in a void that requires the fulfillment of an unmet *need*. These voids are generally *developmental* in nature, and the losses are associated with attachment, trust, or identity issues, for example. A talented therapist addressed my voids in this area by acting as a surrogate father in order to re-enact foundational childhood objectives. Healing occurred through a process called *transference,* a topic described later in this book. Depending on the complexity of voids in this area, you might require the help of a mental health professional.

5) Unfinished Business: When assessing our pasts, most of us find what I call *unfinished business.* These situations usually

involve relationships that feel incomplete because emotions and unspoken truths linger. As a result, they cause various needs for closure, including apologizing, thanking someone, speaking one's peace, and sometimes seeking accountability from someone, a topic we will get to a bit later. One of many such situations for me was my relationship with my father. Not ever having an honest conversation with him, I stuffed all my emotion inside over the years, including anger, confusion, longing, contempt, pity, sadness, and rage. Even when I looked at the few pictures I had of the two of us together, our emotional distance was obvious. I couldn't remember if my father ever hugged me or told me he loved me. On top of my angst, I felt guilty for having so many feelings toward someone who was dead. In order to address this *unfinished business* that was intruding upon my energy and stability, I decided to write him a letter as though he were living and tell him how his behavior affected my life. When I finished the letter, I read it aloud to myself until I

The author, thirteen, with Mike and her father

could do so free of tears. This method allowed me to say and hear my truth – a truth I wasn't aware of or able to express as a child. I believe one of the most vital steps in achieving authenticity is the birth of one's voice, a topic I will discuss later. Because my father was deceased, my choices of communication were more limited than had he been living. This doesn't mean that I would've chosen a different method of communicating with him had he been living, however. Each *unfinished business* situation is unique and needs assessed individually for the best process. The next chapter on communication will be a useful tool when utilizing this type of resolution. My *unfinished business* with my father included multiple losses, including *physical, needs, experiences, expectations, and hope.* The voids produced included *developmental stages, skills, events, knowledge, and relationship.* Today, I still have *unfinished business* in my life, including my relationships with my two sisters and my mother. While I have not communicated with my oldest sister in over a decade, my middle sister and I started communicating again three years ago after a long lapse. Like many topics we have discussed thus far, *unfinished business* is a process and can't be rushed. In chapter thirteen I will discuss how I chose to resolve my *unfinished business* with my mother.

What I have just discussed are different ways to problem solve your childhood losses and their accompanying voids so you can process your grief in a healthy manner and lessen your triggers. This, in turn, frees the energy you once used to hold on to the past for use in the present and future.

🐎 *Exercise 11a: Choose one or two of the losses/voids from your timeline and consider which method of healing you might utilize. Give some thought to how you might proceed but do not begin the process. Some of the information yet to come will help you achieve the healthiest outcome. The 'action' part of this entire process comes after information gathering and enhancing self-awareness as mentioned early-on in this book.*

The process of healing takes whatever time it takes. Remember, you can't hurry grief. Through discovering your past, you may also find clarity with present-day issues that are causing you stress. This next segment speaks to the general practice of healthy problem solving, a skill I believe is rapidly becoming a lost art. Perhaps because the world has become a more complex place in the last twenty-five years with colossal amounts of information and instant everything turning us into human-like spin-wheels, we tend to think we are able to resolve our problems through easy, instant fixes or convenient, cheap, unemotional, feel-good resolutions. While this might sound wonderful, the truth is, humans are more complex than that and most problems demand *and* deserve more from us for the most effective outcomes. One thing that I hope I have conveyed is that when we fail to resolve problems promptly and intelligently, they can accumulate and worsen, eventually plowing us down like a stampede of wild horses. Acquiring problem-solving skills allows you to prevent these self-defeating situations and avoid the accumulation of *guk*.

While I don't profess there to be only one way to arrive at healthy decisions, I have found there are certain factors that successful problem solvers take into consideration. They are *awareness, source,* and *solutions.* But since the use of an acronym here would be, well, a bit distasteful, I have added a fourth factor that I think too few people take into account when making decisions: *consequences*. This makes my acronym ASSC (ask), and with its four letters, I am reminded that I have four topics to consider when solving a problem.

Awareness: Self-awareness is a form of prevention. Though we don't always like to hear it, many of the problems we face in life are human-induced. When we listen to our bodies, we can detect budding intrusion into our healthiness. If someone asked me to steal, for example, I feel an immediate negativity in my body because stealing goes against my belief system. As a result, if I want to maintain authenticity, I need to find the strength to say *no* regardless of how much my mind may begin to rationalize the positive effects. In other words, stealing interferes with who I want to be; it penetrates one of the boundaries of my integrity. If I gave in to the request, my actions would cause me shame, anger, and most likely, regret. So, as much as I hate sounding repetitive, self-knowledge is key to preventive problem solving. If I didn't know my beliefs about stealing, I might make a regrettable, *guk*-producing choice. Awareness is the vital first step in making healthy decisions. To enhance your awareness, inquisitiveness helps. *What, where, why, when,* and *how* are helpful questions if you aren't clear on your boundaries or beliefs. After all, if you don't know what you believe in or why, any action can be problematic.

Source: Once you are aware of an issue, the next step is discovering the source of the problem or, as I like to think of it, *where in the heck did that piece of guk come from?* In our haste, one of the most common mistakes people make in solving problems is jumping to a solution before considering the source of the problem. How many times, for example, have you taken a painkiller without considering the cause of your headache? I know I'm guilty. You just want to get rid of the pain, right? But what if your headache stems from a brain tumor? As we learned with past childhood issues, one of the most important features needed to solve problems is information. The action part of resolving a problem is only as successful as the knowledge base. Consider surgeons. The amount of schooling they acquire is extensive compared to the length of an operation. Anyone can react impulsively to a perceived problem, but healthy, effective solutions come from insightful planning and knowledge. Whether you are looking back at your childhood or forward to your future, taking time to understand a problem is critical and, ultimately, self-serving.

Solutions: Yes, plural. Although we ultimately use only one solution to solve a problem, coming up with at least five possible solutions gives us a greater opportunity for success. Let me explain. Just as you remember teachers telling you *there is no such thing as a stupid question,* I say *there is no such thing as a stupid possible solution.* I call this part of finding solutions *ultimate brainstorming.* But before I go on, let's practice.

Exercise 11b: Write down five solutions to the following problem: While shopping, you think you see your best friend's sixteen-year-old son who has recently joined a gang put a store item in his pocket. As he does this, you think you also see a gun. What do you do?

Ultimate brainstorming challenges us to consider more than one solution. Some people in the above scenario might immediately call the police. Others might tell the store manager, walk away and ignore the fact that they saw anything, or tell the boy's mother. And what about confronting the boy? This problem is a judgment call, as are many problems we encounter. There may not be one *right* answer, but there is probably one *healthier* answer for you given your relationship with the boy's mother, your beliefs, your morals, and safety issues. Thinking of as many solutions as possible is an exercise I do anytime I face an important decision.

Consequences: The last step in solving problems is considering the consequences of each possible solution. Because any action taken can create a trickling effect, it is crucial to try to anticipate what impact your decisions might have. In the prior example, any of the five decisions you make will have an impact. Calling the police, for example, might resolve the situation or it might escalate the situation, especially if what you thought you saw proved to be wrong. Then there is the boy's mother. Depending on what you do, she might thank you or she might end your friendship. The unknowns in this situation are numerous. We don't know if the boy has a weapon, if any of his friends are in the store to back him up, how he would react if confronted, or how the situation would play out if either the police or the store manager were involved. Looking at the possible consequences to potential resolutions plays an important part in solving problems. Only after you have thought out all the possible repercussions can you make an informed decision.

Exercise 11c: Given the five options you considered, weigh the possible consequences. How might each choice change your life, your relationship with your friend, your safety, or your emotional health? Did any of your choices tempt you to act against your values, morals, or beliefs? Which option did you choose and why?

The healthiest individuals I know confront problems as they arise and seek solutions that uphold their integrity. They know that anything less will have an emotional impact on them, causing *guk* in the form of secrets, regret, shame, or mishandled responsibility. Just as a pot of boiling water eventually evaporates and starts a fire, they understand that problems left unattended will most likely intensify. This is what happened to us as children when unhealthy events were not resolved.

The process of ASSC (awareness, source, solutions, and consequences) encourages us to think about our lives as a whole. Knowing who you are and why you do what you do allows for the healthiest long-term outcomes. Do you think the Donner Party's first choice was to eat their fellow travelers? I know. Yuk. But I hope you get my point. Some problems in life generate the need for making difficult decisions. Had the Donner Party done nothing, they probably would have also died.

Much of the success in solving problems comes from maintaining one's integrity through self-honesty. When we make decisions based on thorough consideration of their consequences despite the difficulty they present, it results in fewer internal battles and regrets. Doing what is right instead of what is easy builds character embraced by pride and self-respect. Ultimately, these characteristics serve to promote the greater, healthy good.

What we can all count on is that life will challenge our inner peace. Perhaps we don't have to worry about mischievous talking horses such as Mr. Ed, but our success nonetheless will be dependent upon our ability to healthily solve problems, an *art* well worth performing.

Trail Notes

- U Unresolved problems interfere with our ability to feel authentic

- U Our losses and voids are problems that make up the missing, damaged, and misplaced puzzle pieces from our childhood

- U Rituals, re-enactment, replacement, surrogacy, and unfinished business help us grieve and fill any voids caused by childhood losses

- U Awareness, Source, Solutions, and Consequences (ASSC) stimulates healthy problem solving

- U Ultimate brainstorming helps us to expand our options

Chapter Twelve

I Only Have Words for You

It's all about the Communication

My next therapeutic experience began by accident, literally. Driving home from work one night, I came upon a car with a bloody, shattered windshield straddling the centerline. As I slowed, I noticed a young man getting out of the car and oncoming traffic edging around a disfigured body lying on the pavement. Worried the driver was going to be hit, I stopped my van to block traffic, got out, and redirected the young man to the curb to sit down. After the police and paramedics arrived, I proceeded home, later learning that the victim had been intoxicated when he walked into traffic, his intent unclear. The driver was barely seventeen and not cited. The following day I met therapist Steven C. Kalas when I attended a lecture he was giving on grief. With the accident clouding my mind, I sensed him to be someone I might feel comfortable talking to, so I summoned the courage to ask if I could see him professionally. I began therapy the following week.

As is common, my presenting topic in therapy was not the real issue plaguing me. Talking about the accident allowed me to assess whether or not I wanted to confide my life's story to this particular stranger. Clearly aware of this, Steven listened patiently, allowing me to set the pace. Part of my ability to continue working with him was due to his lack of intrusiveness. Steven had a way of making me *want* to talk, a new and refreshing phenomenon for me.

Prior to therapy, the intensity of my anxiety attacks resulted in my calling 9-1-1. Though not blatantly rude, the paramedics gave me oxygen and then left without explanation. Detecting an annoyance in their demeanor, I later learned as a volunteer for the fire department that mental health calls sat at the bottom of their thrill scale, right alongside child drownings, though for different reasons. When I became a crisis supervisor, the reality of their distaste for "9-18" calls, the code for mental health, evidenced itself as some of the emergency responders resorted to slang terms such as *crazy, loony,* or *nuts,* even in the presence of patients. Despite going against federal regulations, sometimes emergency rooms even refused treatment for mental health patients, forcing me to send crisis mobile teams to assist. One of the psychiatrists I worked with summarized this behavior as an indication of society's ignorance of their own mental health issues. "Never," he said, "would you see such apathy toward someone experiencing a heart attack or suffering from a broken limb." Experiences such as these, coupled with my own, prompted me to gravitate toward advocating appropriate and respectful treatment for patients, something I had not anticipated necessary in our *civilized* society.

In therapy, Steven did not focus on a diagnosis or use clinical terminology. Instead, he respectfully and skillfully listened, paraphrased, validated, and asked questions. He allowed the space we shared to be safe for me to discover my truths without impending judgment. He supported my making sense out of my anger, confusion, depression, and suicidal thoughts. And though I found talking about my life disturbing and exhausting, I grew to trust Steven and spent many nights on the phone with him in an attempt to placate my latest intense emotion. To this day, I attribute the extent of my progress to his willingness to take my calls after hours. I would not have confided in anyone else.

Soon, however, even talking nightly with Steven failed to subdue my demons. The scope of my grief made me feel as if I were on a treadmill set one speed faster than I was capable of running. Between my mental exhaustion, my parenting duties, and working, the demands of my life far outweighed my energy level. As a result, Steven and I debated whether hospitalization might be the best option. Perhaps other people could have avoided such a drastic measure through family support or more financial means, but I had neither. Weeks earlier, sensing my emotional decline, I had swallowed my pride and asked my mother if I could fly her down to watch Gabe and Zach so I could get some rest, but she denied my request. Ultimately, Steven and the CEO at hospice arranged for Gabe and Zach's care while I was in the hospital.

In earlier days, going to a mental health hospital for stabilization purposes was not uncommon. When I went, Steven and I both learned that even with good insurance, admittance was rare unless you posed a danger to yourself or someone else. The admitting nurse disclosed upfront that she could only send me to the *holding room*, an area used to house patients called *frequent flyers* due to their repeated appearances at the hospital without meeting inpatient requirements. Standing in the waiting room after hearing this information, I felt a fleeting bond with Jack Nicholson's rebel character in *One Flew Over the Cuckoo's Nest*, challenging me to expose such preposterous regulations. But, of course, I hadn't the audacity to bring such attention to myself. Still, the concept of being in pain and a hospital not helping unless I tried to hurt myself or someone else staggered me. *Isn't that what I was attempting to prevent?* The outrageousness of my situation further defined itself when staff told me they would monitor my shower due to the razor blade in my possession yet I could keep my purse, which concealed a nail file, a pocketknife, and enough painkillers to sedate a small elephant. Succumbing to that which I had no energy to battle, I spent the extent of my hospital stay on a cot in the corner of a cold room combating chills, sweats, and nausea, a consequence of having to discontinue my anti-depressant medication because their doctor had not prescribed them. The ultimate benefit I gained from my hospitalization was a clearer understanding of what I was up against, both as a patient and future therapist.

Not long after my hospital stay I met Lynn, a new employee at hospice, and her intuition immediately honed in on my internal unrest. Within no time, our relationship grew to that of adopted sisters and we spent endless hours together connecting at a depth I hadn't imagined possible. Strengthening our bond was us each having two sons about the same ages and, except for her husband, no other family nearby. Lynn's presence in my life allowed me to see what my life had been missing, and I craved our *family* time, especially the holiday celebrations that we planned together for our children. Lynn was one of those *once in a lifetime* friends who graciously and unexpectedly appears in one's life when most unexpected yet needed. Her gentle spirit and innate kindness allowed me to feel a part of something special that was previously lacking. For the first time, I didn't feel alone in my pain.

Just because you say something doesn't mean the other person hears what you thought you said. Confused? Well, perhaps novelist Fyodor Dostoyevsky said it best: "Much unhappiness has come into the world

CHAPTER TWELVE

because of bewilderment and things left unsaid." The truth is, there's a whole lot that can go wrong between a person's words and how they are interpreted. Sometimes we immediately know when this happens. Other times, the consequences of the miscommunication do not materialize until later on, when problems arise. Such was the case when two of my girlfriends and I set a lunch date for *Thursday*. Yep, you got it. I thought we were talking about the same week and they meant the following week. Waiting at the restaurant, I eventually realized what had happened. The upside? I enjoyed two restaurant meals instead of one. Unfortunately, an upside doesn't always materialize. Too often the miscommunication trickles into more misconstrued messages, creating a time bomb of problems.

Miscommunication occurs more often than we realize or like to admit. Numerous times in family therapy I witness the evolution of effective communication as no less astonishing than a magical act in Vegas, beginning as a sort of contemporary Abbott and Costello's *Who's on First* reality show and transforming into the type of precision depicted by trapeze artists. In the end, I can say it no better than this: *Effective communication is priceless*. Truly. It costs nothing except effort. The price tag of failure, however, is extensive. Consider this: the style in which you communicate influences your life's successes.

Think back for a moment. Your ability to communicate words probably began with *ma…ma,* albeit prejudicially fed to you by your mother. From there, as though a parrot, you repeated other parental-chosen words. "Oh, how cute is that," they bragged to their friends. Then the cuteness wore off when you mimicked other overheard phrases such as *I want, No!* and, all too often, *&%!#!*.

Exercise 12a: How would you describe your communication style? What method of communicating do you prefer best: talking, writing, face-to-face, telephone, email, texting, or Skype? Why? What is your least favorite? Again, why? Consider any feedback you receive when communicating, whether it is "you're a good listener" to "please don't interrupt me" to "say something!" In a typical month, how often do you resort to silence in order to avoid perceived confrontation and how often do you yell in order to get your point across? Do you ever regret any of the things you say?

Each of your answers to the above questions tells you something about your communication style. Remember, awareness is the first step to changing something that isn't working. The only shame involved in acknowledging our weaknesses is if we then don't attempt to strengthen them. If you find yourself in that scenario, consider asking yourself why. *Why would I not want to decrease my stress, improve my relationships, and have more power in my life with which to achieve my goals?* Imagine that your dreams are but one effective communication away. Okay, quick quiz. Ready? What is one of the most powerful skills in life? You got it! *Communication.*

Wrought with secrecy and silence is the best way I can describe my communication style prior to therapy. I was adept at keeping my thoughts to myself, a behavior founded by my introverted personality but strengthened by a childhood culture that stunted my social development. I have always processed tons of information in my head, but early on in life I learned to keep my thoughts to myself. The result of this mal-adapted communication style was that getting to know me was quite difficult. If I felt forced to talk, the product of my internal editing resulted in nondescript and closed-ended statements such as *yes, no,* or *I don't know*. Besides not feeling as though I had anything of value to say, I also had little interest in what other people had to say. Yes, this demeanor made me come across arrogant, aloof, and self-centered. Had

CHAPTER TWELVE

anyone attempted to understand my presentation, however, the reason for my behavior might have been uncovered. Usually, though, people react to behavior without giving any thought to its origin. And it is this failure to question the *why,* particularly with children, that results in overlooking crucial information.

You've no doubt seen the movie where a woman is held hostage with a gun to her back but has to answer the door and get rid of the police so she isn't harmed. She talks with her eyes. *Help me. There is a deranged man behind me with a gun*, although her actual monotone words are the unconvincing, "No officer, I'm fine." So, what wins out, the verbal or non-verbal message? Have you ever heard the saying, *Actions speak louder than words?* Well, research by Albert Mehrabian shows just that. The influence of the non-verbal portion of a communication is often more powerful than the actual words, especially when the two contradict each other. "How can that be?" you ask.

Well, anyone who negates the power of non-verbal communication has undoubtedly never owned a basset hound. My son, Zach, was sixteen when we went searching for his Christmas present. You guessed it. A basset hound. Fred, as he became known, soon grew into a seventy pound, four-foot-long hound with extra-long ears, big feet, and a huge heart. He also became the neediest dog I have ever owned. Incidentally, I inherited Fred when Zach went off to college and lived in a house with a pool. Side note: bassets sink. So, to put it bluntly, Fred has not had the best of luck in life. To begin with, he was born with deformed front legs that required surgery around his first birthday. Then, he *bloated,* an often fatal condition that occurs when the stomach twists. Another surgery. Soon after that another dog beat him up. Surgery again. Then a hip problem. Yep, surgery. Next, he was diagnosed with valley fever, Cushing's disease, and hyperthyroidism, three conditions requiring lifetime medications. Had I any type of intuition, pet

Fred, the "million-dollar" dog

insurance would have been a bargain. We now call Fred our million-dollar dog, though his worth is actually beyond measure. But let's get back to non-verbal communication.

Fred can say more with his big brown eyes in one longing gaze than most of us do in a fifteen-minute conversation. Probably the only reason Fred survived the night he bloated was due to his excellence at playing charades. Relaxing on the couch snuggling my canines as is common in my less than socially prominent Saturday evenings, I noticed Fred had been outside for quite some time. Another side note: bassets are couch potatoes, so this was odd. When I went to check on him, I found him with his nose to the ground making strange noises attempting to back up. When our eyes finally met, his big browns said it all: *Help me!* So off to the emergency clinic we went. At four in the morning, the veterinarian told me surgery was a success.

Fred's ability to communicate, however, is not limited to his body language. As if a cell phone with different ring tones, Fred has different howl sounds and an envious volume range that allows me to know when I should be worried. Such was the time I ran outside and found him face-to-face with a rattlesnake, prompting me to lasso him with a rope in order to drag him to safety. Have I mentioned that basset hounds are a bit stubborn when they find something intriguing? Only once have I seen Fred move away from a critter voluntarily, and that was after he cornered a tarantula that reared up on its hind legs and spat at him. Being a macho basset hound, I'm sure Fred would dispute this, but I'm pretty sure I heard him whimper.

One of the reasons non-verbal communication prevails over verbal communication, especially when they fail to complement each other, is because non-verbal communication is more honest. I can change the words I say quite easily, but because so much of non-verbal communication is instinctual, altering it is more difficult. Learning to have control over one's eye movements, body posture, and voice tone takes dedication. Actors study these skills intensely so they can accurately portray their characters. Most of the rest of us are relatively unaware of all the non-verbal cues we give, allowing for some of our communication to cause confusion. *Words are cheap* is a common phrase I'm sure you've heard when someone says something with little sincerity or doesn't follow-up with compatible actions. Families that communicate in unclear messages complicate healthy development. An interesting aspect about communication is this: you can use non-verbal language without the verbal, but you cannot use verbal language without non-verbal influence. The moment you speak a word your voice tone alone affects the meaning, and when your verbal and non-verbal fail to mesh, there is room for misinterpretation.

For clarity, let me say that both words and actions have the ability to deliver strong messages. Despite the saying *Sticks and stones may break my bones but words will never hurt me,* words *can* hurt, leaving painful wounds and shredding self-esteem. Communication is powerful, no matter the form, and it influences us from the moment we are born.

Along with *verbal* and *non-verbal* components, the third element affecting communication is *listening*. Whenever I witness two people struggling to understand each other, I think of the movie *Rush Hour* where Jackie Chan states in slow motion, "D o   y o u   h e a r   t h e   w o r d s t h a t a r e c o m i n g o u t o f m y   m o u t h ?" and I can't help but laugh. This *listening* stuff seems so easy. In order to listen effectively, though, you not only have to take both the verbal and nonverbal into account, but you also have to interpret the message given your current mood and worldview. If that isn't challenging enough, most of us try to formulate a response as we are listening as well.

I did not become aware of the acuteness of my communication deficits until I began therapy. Although I had a degree in speech communications, I never really *liked* to talk. It felt unnatural to me. One of the first questions I asked my therapist was even a flippant, "And how is talking going to help me?" My failure to learn the benefits of communication were long standing. Although I envied people who talked comfortably and genuinely, for me speaking was painful and challenging. For the majority of my life, I avoided speaking unless it was necessary. Even when the phone rang, I let the answering machine pick it up, one time prompting a visit from the police when someone was worried about me. Not until I became a supervisor for our county's twenty-four-hour crisis phone line – yes, there is some irony there – did I face my communication shortfall.

Not knowing where to begin to improve my skills, I came up with three easy rules I could use in order to communicate effectively: honesty, respectfulness, and directness. I wish the acronym was more exciting, but the best I could come up with is HRD, and I think of it as short for *heard*. The key to HRD is using all three components at the same time. I know many people, for example, who pride themselves on their honesty. Unfortunately, they spew their truth disrespectfully or indirectly. In Texas, they have a saying regarding this: *Speak your truth but ride a fast horse*. Other people communicate respectfully, though they say what they think the person wants to hear rather than their truth. I will admit that utilizing

HRD can be challenging at times, but the reward is that it minimizes miscommunication and decreases the creation of *guk*.

I first began practicing HRD at work. Each time I needed to communicate, I thought about what I wanted to say and questioned myself before speaking to make sure I was being honest, respectful, and direct. Situations where I may have remained silent in the past became opportunities to speak my mind because I had guidelines to follow that made it easier. As with most new skills, the more I practiced the more comfortable and skilled I became. In time, I challenged myself to find a conversation that would not benefit from the directives of HRD. The only circumstance I have found so far is an emergency that requires immediate attention to ensure someone's safety without regard for anyone's feelings being hurt. Otherwise, HRD is a format I have found to be of value in all situations, whether business, personal, or social.

HRD is also one of the tools I began using in my private practice to teach families how to improve their relationships. Because flawed communication is at the root of many problems, families who utilize HRD discover that some of their ongoing issues automatically disappear as they treat each other kinder through improved communication skills. As you begin to problem solve your childhood losses and voids, HRD is a tool that can also assist you. For example, when I addressed my *unfinished business* and wrote the letter to my father, HRD guided me in being able to say what I needed to without feeling I was coming across uncaring or vindictive. Overall, HRD makes upholding one's integrity easier because honesty, respect, and directness dictate accountability and healthiness. Although the recipient of your message may disagree with your *honesty* when you use HRD, there is little room to fault its delivery when directness and respectfulness found the message. Two important thoughts: some communication is necessary even if not pleasant to deliver, and honest communication is about speaking one's truth, not finding agreement from the recipient.

🐾 *Exercise 12b: Consider the following scenario: Your best friend promises to bring dessert for an important gathering you are having, but then doesn't show up and doesn't bother to call you. Later you run into her at the grocery store. How do you think you would feel? What do you think you would say to her?*

While HRD sets the guidelines for healthy communication, the most critical factor encompassing its use is making sure the proposed communication has *purpose with integrity*. If I wanted to tell you, "Your shirt is ugly," for example, I would probably have difficulty finding a *purpose with integrity* for doing so, even if I did so honestly, respectfully, and directly. Such a statement serves no purpose other than to be hurtful. Healthy communication serves a healthy function.

A discussion on communication would not be complete without discussing two extreme forms used in our society: silence and yelling. I am not a fan of silence as a substitute for words that someone is simply unwilling to utilize. Silence is a powerful communication that has the potential to punish, scorn, demean, humiliate, and patronize. Sometimes silence is worse than saying something negative because the ultimate message is *You are not worthy of my time or energy*. In most instances, I believe having the courage to find honest, respectful words and directing them at the person in question has much more value to both people if, of course, there is also a purpose with integrity.

Having said that, silence sometimes serves a need, such as giving people time to collect their thoughts, or when you want to be with someone for support where words aren't necessary. I have also seen silence used as an effective parenting tool after giving instructions to a child twice. In order to make it a beneficial communication, however, the parent needs to discuss the incident with the child afterwards for teaching purposes. Silence is a communication tool requiring careful practice to ensure its respectful use. When I find myself in a situation where I am tempted to remain silent because what I want to say at that moment lacks integrity, I'll say, "I need some time to think about how I want to respond to what you said." This gives me time to think about how I can say what I want to using HRD instead of allowing silence to be my default form of communication. And this brings me to another problematic form of communication.

I am also not a fan of yelling as a healthy means of communication. I've never quite understood why whatever needs said can't be stated in a normal tone of voice. If it's emphasis someone wants, then perhaps change the word choice. Yes, loudness can get the attention of people easier than a normal talking voice, but then, so can a whisper. Try it sometime. If you have to do either in order to get someone's attention, however, there just might be a bigger issue needing resolution. I have been around people whose baseline appears to be yelling. When that is the case, the impact of the emphasis has been lost, so why yell? Even when in a disagreement, does yelling really help the outcome? Not usually. The person yelling might feel better for having released pent-up energy, but too often the words that accompany yelling cause longer-lasting damage. In my experience, yelling is often a result of unprocessed anger, not knowing how to express oneself respectfully, or feeling unheard. Utilizing the guidelines of HRD can help in all these areas.

Exercise 12c: Think back to the last exercise and to what you decided to say to your friend. Now, assess whether you used the three rules of communication (HRD). If not, see if you can re-phrase your statement using HRD. Try to imagine yourself as your friend and feel the difference in the two responses. If you have had any conversations in the recent past that have not gone well, think about how you might have communicated differently using HRD. From this point on, try to incorporate HRD into your life. My experience has been that you won't be sorry.

The most profound gain I received from utilizing HRD was finding my voice. I can't think of anything more empowering than knowing how to verbalize what I want to say based on my beliefs without accruing more *guk*. Throughout my learning process, I came to realize that how people communicate is their strongest asset or their largest liability, and the only difference between the two is knowledge, practice, and desire. My hope is that we will one day embrace healthier treatment of each other through communication so we can reap the benefits of a gentler, more compassionate world. I have no doubt that this skill alone would generate colossal positive change.

After therapy, I made a pledge to myself to use HRD exclusively. What provoked this promise, I might add, was a vivid nightmare wherein Dr. Phil appeared and reiterated a number of my catastrophic communication incidents. Upon finishing his portrayal of my problematic style of conversing, he calmly looked at me and, in his prominent Southern drawl, inquired, "So, how's that working for you?"

Need I say more?

CHAPTER TWELVE

Trail Notes

⋃ The only thing between you and effective communication is practice

⋃ Verbal and non-verbal communication need to complement each other for accurate interpretation; *listening* is a valuable skill

⋃ Used together, Honesty, Respectfulness, and Directness (HRD) promote effective communication

⋃ Having a *purpose with integrity* founds healthy communication

⋃ How you communicate affects every aspect of your life

Chapter Thirteen

Stairway to Freedom

Victims, Blame, and Forgiveness

What steady footing I'd gained collapsed when, within a month of each other, Lynn moved back to her home state of Minnesota and Steven accepted a new job in Nevada. The reality of my two lifelines leaving substantiated that I was far from healed, triggering rage and a profound sadness I have not since equaled. I felt similar to the school geek who thought the popular clique finally accepted her, only to discover it was a prank. Unlike other difficult experiences from which I was able to gain valuable lessons, I blocked the idea of this being an opportunity for growth. Though understanding no one was to blame, a sense of betrayal and unfairness overwhelmed me. *How could this happen?* The question tormented me. *I'm doing my part. I'm going to therapy and facing my truths.* But as much as I struggled to take the disappointment in stride as I felt *normal* people would, I couldn't overcome the feeling that Lynn and Steven were choosing to leave *me*, a conclusion born from my multitude of losses and unresolved voids.

Illogically, I assumed that I understood grief because I worked for a hospice. More accurately was that my intellectual knowledge proved a poor substitute for needing to feel my emotions. Reverting to avoidance, I focused on the only thing I felt I had power over: a pending trip with my sons to the East Coast. With my continued *now or never* conviction, I wanted Gabe and Zach to experience life, to gain insight into how other people lived, and to witness the world. Attempting to fulfill these goals gave me purpose, though more than that, I felt an innate responsibility to do so.

Ignoring all else, I planned our trip hoping to generate unforgettable memories. By its end, we had crammed ourselves atop the Empire State Building to watch Fourth of July fireworks, sailed off the coast of Maine with Gabe navigating the boat, and toured The White House for Zach who was in his *I'm going to be president someday* phase. Not knowing its future significance, we also visited the Twin Towers and looked out over spectacular Manhattan Island and beyond.

Arriving home with a wardrobe of tourist-attraction tee-shirts, reality emerged when the postal worker delivered the consequences of

Zach, ten and Gabe, twelve, sailing in Maine

my escape from reality: bills. Having acquired my first credit cards only prior to our trip, my inexperience with budgeting became unmistakable. With required payments well outside my income, I attempted credit counseling, though this remedy came too late, leaving bankruptcy my most viable option. Feeling numb and defeated, I then had to face Lynn and Steven's departures.

When I thought of Lynn leaving, a deep emptiness and penetrating pain engulfed my body. Had I acted on my emotion, I would have put my arms around her and told her how much she meant to me, threatening never to let go. But I was as yet unable to demonstrate such honesty. By the time she left, neither one of us said good-bye to the other. I had alienated her, unable to look past my pain to try to understand her needs. Returning to my learned skill of evading what I didn't want to feel, I stuffed my grief with the rest of my *guk* and pretended she never existed. Not until years later after completing therapy and facing my *unfinished business* did I contact her and apologize for my behavior. And although she forgave me, the most regrettable loss in my life endures. Second chances, I learned, are not always possible, and I had no one to blame but myself.

With Steven, my grief took a more traditional role, from denial to anger to bargaining to acceptance, encompassing a lengthy and painful journey that took years to complete. As much as I just wanted to give up on therapy altogether, I knew I wasn't ready to let go of him. This meant, despite the unease, continuing to see Steven until he moved. Realizing that nothing I said would change his pending departure, I remained silent, though every time I saw him the wrath beneath my vocal cords threatened to detonate as if an exploding bomb. I had yet to learn that talking was necessary for healing and not a means by which to manipulate a desired outcome. Void of words, my outlet became writing, and poems of fury, despair, and sorrow poured from my heart. One of them I named *The Demon,* and it depicts the mental fight between my *guk* (the demon) and my authenticity (hope).

The Demon

*Back into a world I fall
where shame assaults my highest truth;
where logic lies, subjecting fear,
that breeds self-hate with intense despair.*

*In the past I would cringe and submit to you
the weakness of a frightened child, whose thoughts would
stray so easily to death,
Yes, it is a miracle I survived.*

*But now my vow is to speak honestly —
a fidelity to self, though your
avenging threats ravage my goal
as you taunt and dismiss me as a profound-less soul.*

*Just how conceited must you be
to believe you can rape my integrity
that you can step into my life so free
and inflict envy in hopes of destroying a relationship significant to me.*

*How dare you subject me to your disrespect
of a spirit so well dressed
and haunt me by your insidiousness
assuming my life to be some thing worth less.*

*I'll give you this — you do your job well
for this suffering you induce does feel like hell;
But remember, no matter what forms your deceit
my faith is in myself, my humanness to meet.*

By the time my supervisor asked if I wanted to introduce Steven at his farewell gathering at hospice, I saw the opportunity as one that would enable me to speak my truth but, because it was in front of about a hundred people, I'd also have to do so politely. Interestingly, public speaking was easier for me than a one-on-one conversation, as well as further evidence of my attachment deficits. I didn't worry about revealing our therapeutic relationship because, although it was subtle, I hadn't been treated the same since my hospital stay. Perhaps because of this I felt even more compelled to speak my peace. I practiced my speech on my way to work each day until I could recite it nearly automatically and, more importantly, tearless, which also provided me with a means by which to grieve. After my talk, numerous people told me of their own stories of child abuse, depression, and grief, and thanked me for sharing. Surprised by this response, I realized I was not alone in my journey and the idea that speaking my truth was more important than maintaining my privacy was born. Though I had a long way to go, an inner determination materialized that day that would not go away anytime soon, and not long thereafter, I began writing this book.

After a dire attempt to keep our therapeutic relationship alive, my relationship with Steven faded and the few times we spoke felt tense and unnatural. Eventually, as I gained power over my *guk* with a new therapist, I was able to view his departure as something other than stemming from my unworthiness. Today, Steven is my mentor, and I feel honored to be able to continue to benefit from his wisdom. Had anyone told me that I would survive my grief and arrive at such a place, I probably would have laughed. At the time, all I knew was that the only person I had ever trusted to help me was leaving, and that life was unjust and deceptive.

I was in grade school the first time I saw the painting *Christina's World* by Andrew Wyeth. The scene is a barren field in Maine where a young woman is laying on the ground longing toward a distant farmhouse. The painting is said to have been inspired by Wyeth's mourning of his father. For me, *Christina's World* depicted my crippled wholeness — an outcast attempting to reach the illusion of *home*. Not yet ten years old, I already characterized myself as blameworthy even though I was unclear what I had done wrong; not yet realized was that first and foremost, I was a victim.

> *Exercise 13a: When you hear the word "victim", what is your first thought? How would you define the word? Write down your answers on your timeline.*

There are many reasons why children require a guardian until the age of eighteen. One reason is that children need help processing the difference between healthy and unhealthy. Short of this guidance, a child can misinterpret the world, allowing for the development of faulty beliefs and dysfunctional behavior. This is what occurred with the girl in chapter one when she watched her father hit her mother. Without anyone to intervene, she grew up believing that hitting was *normal*. When situations such as this one occur, a child becomes a victim: *someone adversely affected by an action or circumstance*. This girl became a *victim* of a domestic violence household due to the lack of accountability by her parents. While we often think the term *victim* describes only those in extreme circumstances such as physical or sexual abuse, the reality is all children are potential victims of imperfect childhoods simply by virtue of the humanness of parents and the inequities that persist in life. What differentiates those who are *adversely affected* from those who aren't is often how parents respond to the *action* or *circumstance* in question. In other words, if the mother in the domestic violence example had explained to her daughter that her father's actions were wrong and subsequently protected her from such an environment, the child would have had an opportunity to develop a different worldview. Children are vulnerable when unhealthiness occurs in their lives and, when no one responds to that unhealthiness effectively, becoming a victim is a potential outcome.

A poignant example in one of my favorite movies, *Ordinary People*, portrays how a mother victimizes her son. The movie unfolds with dad, mom, and teenage son in the aftermath of a sailing accident that took the life of the eldest son. The mother pretends everything is fine, though her internal rage evidences itself through tense, ambiguous communication aimed toward her surviving son. Blaming himself for not being able to save his brother, the surviving son has just arrived home from the hospital after attempting suicide. Meanwhile, the father puts his grief on hold in order to try to help his wife and son mend their relationship. Beautifully directed by Robert Redford, the movie embodies many lessons, including how easily a child can take on blame when a parent lacks accountability, the power of the truth, the inability to change other people if they don't want to change, the importance of parental emotional healthiness, and the necessity of setting boundaries for emotional self-protection against unhealthy environments.

Exercise 13b: Look at the losses on your timeline and underline any you consider your fault. Next to each of these, write a short statement explaining why you think you are blameworthy.

One of the unfortunate facts surrounding the word *victim* is its negative connotation. Despite my love of the Old West, I draw the line at our society's prevailing John Wayne mentality of toughness and the accompanying *get over it*, *buck up*, and *be a man* attitude. These and all the other quips indicating humans should ignore suffering work against healthiness. *Victim* is a fitting term for those harmed through unhealthy events, just as *grieving* is the minister for healing such occurrences. Without acknowledging our injury, inner peace will no doubt elude us. *Victim*, I attest, is not a *dirty* word.

After working with hundreds of victims through my positions as crisis supervisor, therapist, foster parent, and mental health advocate, as well as having been a victim myself, my conclusion is this: I have yet to meet anyone who enjoys being a victim. Our society tends to judge people on what I call *victim mentality* – patterns of behavior that promote helplessness – and fail to understand that people rarely get to this unpleasant, powerless place by choice. I suggest most victims fall into one of the following three categories:

1) They don't know they are a *victim* (lack of awareness),

2) They know they are a *victim* but don't know how not to be (ignorance), or

3) They know they are a *victim* but pretend not to be (fear of facing the truth).

Initially, the surviving son in *Ordinary People* does not understand he is a victim. Without this awareness, he blames himself for his mother's estrangement from him. Perhaps the most telling comment in the movie comes when his therapist offers an alternative to his self-blame by proposing that his mother is unable to love him any more than she does. This isn't meant as an excuse, but as validation that he is a victim of his mother's unhealthiness, a concept he had not considered. Confirmation of his victimization occurs when his mother impulsively tells him she feels the wrong son died. As hurtful as her statement is, this dispelling of her truth ultimately allows the son to begin healing.

The truth possesses power often beyond our comprehension. Until we reveal and stand by our truths, any attempt to resolve our suffering will most likely fail. Such is the premise behind therapy. When I first began speaking publicly about childhood healing, a close friend gave me the following advice, "If you don't want anyone to disagree with you, don't open your mouth." Whenever I think about that statement, I can't help but smile because it reminds me that my truth is not about seeking agreement. My truth is about permeating peace and power within myself. As you discover your truths, a similar enlightenment is bound to occur. This insight is the epitome of the *freedom* that Alice Miller speaks of in *The Truth Will Set You Free*. Becoming a victim during childhood is out of a child's control; facing that victimization in adulthood is a choice.

Near the end of *Ordinary People,* the evidence of the father and son having faced their truths is visible through their diminished inner conflict and ability to move forward in their lives. The mother, on the other hand, remains stagnant. This leaves the father and son with having to form some difficult boundaries in order to ensure their continued emotional healthiness. The significance of the movie's title also bears mentioning. This father, mother, and son *are* ordinary. We all face issues in life that challenge us to face our truths. Whether or not we accept these challenges determines the course of our lives.

Exercise 13c: Have you ever faced any difficult past truths? What were some of the consequences of your experiences? Are you aware of any past truths that you are ignoring? Do any of them feel like secrets? If so, consider adding these to your guk bag.

This brings us to blame, a topic that also bears a negative undertone, but often for legitimate reasons. Blames means: *to find fault with, to place responsibility, or to criticize.* Sadly, we excel at this in our country. Just watch how often our politicians accuse the other side of some wrongdoing. Or, listen to the defenses that come out of a person's mouth when something bad happens. "It wasn't my fault!" Many even call us a *blame-happy* society – a label substantiated by our plethora of lawsuits – insinuating that we have difficulty accepting the humanness in making mistakes and, more so, in taking responsibility for them. This makes understanding blame pertinent to your success, as some of the experiences on your trail ride may pertain to this complex subject.

By its use alone, blaming is generally not an effective method to resolve issues from your past. That's not to say that it won't be a *part* of your path to authenticity. Simply criticizing or telling people they did wrong, however, lacks one of the ingredients of healthy communication: *purpose with integrity.* In other words, if you think you find a blameworthy circumstance in your childhood, it is not only important to know *why* you want to place blame, but it is also important to understand *how* blaming someone will promote your wholeness. To blame without purpose can result in the accumulation of more *guk*. Healthy reasons for blaming usually involve *accountability*. We want someone to acknowledge our childhood losses – to take responsibility – to validate our victimization. We want someone to tell us it wasn't our fault – that we were children whose needs didn't get met – that our *normal* wasn't *healthy*. But before I go on, let's back up for a moment.

Issues of blame are best left until near the end of your trail ride. The reason for this is that preparation and clarity are essential for success. Although the desire to blame may occur at any time along your journey, applying the lessons in this book first allows for any unwarranted blame to dissipate. Underneath the desire to *criticize, find fault, or place responsibility* are emotions that first need interpreted. Sometimes our idea of who is responsible for a particular childhood loss is blurred by *guk*, similar to how we might have acquired false self-blame. Gaining

CHAPTER THIRTEEN

clarity on the big picture of your childhood makes the decision of *to blame or not to blame* a less difficult one.

When you reach the point where you have a thorough sense of your childhood story, you will find your unresolved issues of blame waiting for you in your *unfinished business* category, along with any other unsettled matters. From there, the use of ASSC (awareness, source, solutions, and consequences) can help you determine what action to take, if any, and any necessary communication can be assisted through HRD (honesty, respectfulness, and directness). In just a moment I will share how I handled the issues of blame and accountability with my mother. A critical point to remember: The question isn't whether blaming and seeking accountability can be a valuable endeavor; the question is whether you have set yourself up for the success you deserve.

Exercise 13d: In exercise 13b you underlined the losses you thought were your fault. Return to these and consider if anyone could've prevented these losses. My losses, for example, stemmed from my unhealthy experiences with my father. For quite some time I blamed myself for these. I believed I was the wrong gender, not likeable, and a burden. As I looked at my childhood using PAS (processing a story), however, I realized that it was not my job as a child to understand and compensate for my father's shortcomings. I then questioned who could have prevented these losses, or who was ultimately responsible. I came up with two people: my father and my mother.

I know a woman who spends every Thanksgiving with her mother and father pretending to have a good time despite knowing the man she eats turkey next to raped her numerous times growing up. When she confided in her mother at the time of the first sexual assault, her mother told her she was disrespecting her father by making up such stories. Feeling shamed, the girl kept the subsequent rapes a secret. Now, every year around Thanksgiving, this woman seeps into a deep depression, cuts her arms for emotional release, and contemplates suicide due to the triggers that haunt her.

I tell this story because it represents many accountings I have heard over the years that validate the power parents hold over their children, even in adulthood. To an emotionally healthy person, the idea of sitting next to your rapist sounds ludicrous. Even this woman's *authentic* self knows the absurdity of the situation; unfortunately, her voice lies buried under her *guk*, unable to break free due to fearing the price is too steep. There is painful ambivalence in feeling you must choose between your family and your true self. And yet, this is a common dilemma in our society. Although the parental-child bond is undoubtedly the strongest of all human ties, it is significant to state that this bond is not automatically healthy. Messages such as *Honor thy parents, Parents know best,* and *Children should be seen and not heard* prompt children to feel they have to resort to silence and self-blame for the unhealthiness in their lives because they feel their parents are off limits. It is *most illogical,* as Star Trek's Spock might say, that children must face such vast society-imposed obstacles despite what we as a nation profess we want: to raise healthy children.

I speak to societal biases regarding children because they can make seeking accountability a tremendous challenge. When I decided to face my mother, just the thought of bringing up the past made me feel as though I was doing something wrong. I knew it made therapeutic sense, but fear dominated me as if I were plotting to devalue *The Pledge of Allegiance*. It felt un-American. Society's subliminal messages kept deterring my action. Sadly, this is often the case when adults need to challenge the behavior of their childhood authority figures such as parents, teachers, coaches, church elders, community leaders, and relatives. That's why I advocate for preparedness.

When I finally decided to approach my mother, it was after immense reassuring self-talk and groundwork. "Are you sure you want to do this?" the message in my head repeated. And each time I had to dig a little deeper to find the voice that could prevail over my mother's rule. As with my father, I chose to write my mother a letter since she lived a thousand miles away. I didn't want to put her on the spot by calling her. If she chose to respond, I wanted her to have time to think about what she wanted to say to me. Part of my preparation was brainstorming all the *guk* that I felt stood in the way of us having a healthy relationship. Then I summed it up. *Why didn't my mother protect me from my father?* As a therapist, I understood that my father was an addict and that, simply, he chose booze over me. Although this didn't excuse his behavior, it did make him easier to understand. I also accepted that parents make mistakes and that it is always easier in hindsight to say, "I should have…" or "I wish I would've…" Yet, my mother had never initiated a discussion with me regarding my childhood. I didn't even know if she felt any responsibility for what happened to me.

I began my letter with the essay and introduction to this book, *Obsolete*, in hopes it would allow her insight into my experience as a child. I then told her I felt angry, sad, and disconnected from her because I didn't understand why she allowed my father to care for me when she knew he had a drinking problem. The purpose of my letter was to expel the *guk* I had been carrying around by exposing the secret that we had never discussed – my victimization. This course of action is known as *giving back that which doesn't belong to you.* As a child, I had inherited the burden of blame because no other explanation was given for the deficits in our family. My letter told a different story. For the first time in our relationship, I voiced my truth, inviting my mother to do the same.

The reality of addressing accountability is that you can't demand someone accept responsibility, and not everyone is ready or willing to speak their truth. This makes defensive responses and additional victimization a possibility. For this reason, part of my preparation was making sure I was strong enough to handle any negative impact that might come with my mother's response. To help with this, I used something called *the worst case scenario,* an exercise that involves thinking of as many outcomes as possible and figuring out how best to handle each one in case it occurred. This gave me added confidence to write what was necessary despite its difficulty. But, before I discuss my mother's reply to my letter, let's talk about forgiveness.

Exercise 13e: What are your beliefs regarding forgiveness? What is forgiveness? What does healthy forgiveness look like? What is the goal of forgiveness? Add these answers to your timeline.

In order to make healthy decisions when it comes to forgiveness, we first need to understand the importance of boundaries. While I have touched on this topic previously, it is worth repeating that boundaries are what protect us from acquiring *guk*. Boundaries incorporate everything in life. Land has boundaries, jobs have boundaries, and laws uphold boundaries. A boundary is *the point at which something ends or beyond which it becomes something else.* Healthy people incorporate boundaries into their lives to protect themselves physically and emotionally. Pretend there is a huge bubble encompassing your body. You have the power to decide what you let into your bubble. If your ultimate goal is maintaining authenticity, healthiness, and peace in your life, your decisions regarding your boundaries need to uphold these guidelines. Let's look at food as a simple example. If you are allergic to peanuts and don't want to become ill, you are going to ban peanuts from your bubble. Less concrete examples occur when trying to protect your emotional healthiness. Are you going to let people in your bubble who keep secrets from you? Bully you? Negatively trigger you? Disrespect you? Your bubble allows you to think about the power you have over your life so you can make decisions regarding your personal happiness. As a child, you didn't always have the power to set your own boundaries. As an adult, you do.

Now to forgiveness: Forgiveness is *the act of pardoning somebody for a mistake or wrongdoing.* I am not here to tell you who to forgive and who not to forgive. My goal is for you to understand the realm of forgiveness so you won't be misguided into thinking that telling someone you forgive them is necessary in order to heal childhood losses or that the outcome of forgiveness will automatically fulfill the voids you are grieving. Forgiveness is another complex topic that, similar to blame, must begin with acknowledging your truths.

In general, forgiveness means you have chosen to cease resentment, indignation, or anger toward somebody for a mistake or wrongdoing. There are also some myths about forgiveness that we will discuss. Understanding your options will help you make decisions from a place of knowledge and integrity rather than fallacy or emotion.

I have found that there are two means of healthy forgiveness: *shared forgiveness* and *solo forgiveness*. *Shared forgiveness* can only occur when the wrongdoer is accountable and apologizes to the victim. In return, the victim accepts the apology and *forgives* the person. *Solo forgiveness,* on the other hand, occurs when the victim chooses not to confront the person, or the wrongdoer fails to show accountability, is not approachable, or is deceased.

Some misconceptions in our society regarding *forgiveness* are longstanding. One common myth is the phrase, *Forgive and forget.*

Forget? Really? How do you do that? I mean, really. If *shared* forgiveness has occurred, there should be no need for *forgetting*. Okay, perhaps both parties chose not to bring the topic up again, but to *forget* past offenses carries with it the potential for making a person unnecessarily vulnerable. Forget? Not really even possible without memory loss.

The second myth surrounding forgiveness is that *reconciliation* occurs at the same time. Wrong. *Forgiving* does not mean the relationship will return to its pre-offensive state. That, too, is not possible. Relationships move forward, not backward. Reconciliation *can* occur, of course, and is often a natural outcome in healthy, ongoing relationships such as friendships and marriages. Other times, however, shared or solo forgiveness occurs without the intent or choice of reconciliation. I knew a couple once who went to therapy after losing their daughter in a bicycle accident. Each week they sat next to each other and apologized for their role, yet the incident had torn the couple apart and neither had an interest in staying together. It was, perhaps, one of the most touching examples of shared forgiveness I have heard about, yet the relationship ended. Reconciliation is a choice, not a mandate of forgiveness.

As we discuss forgiveness, here are a few things to remember:

1) Grieving and discovering the truth need to be completed prior to forgiveness.

2) Premature forgiveness can cause resentment.

3) As with the concept of *giving back that which doesn't belong to you*, forgiveness is an act void of behavior that attempts to manipulate a certain outcome.

4) If forgiveness is not genuine, emotional peace rarely follows.

5) There are no shortcuts to healthy grieving.

In *Ordinary People*, the son was not able to engage in shared forgiveness with his mother because she chose to avoid her truths. Instead, the son felt forced to set boundaries around his mother in order to protect his emotional well-being.

My life took a similar path. In my mother's response, she questioned the accuracy of certain details in my essay that were irrelevant to the story's message, such as the color of my blanket. Respecting her polite avoidance of my reason for writing, I chose not to press the issue, although the child in me wanted to scream, "Why won't you hear me!" Having readied myself for a variety of outcomes, I knew this one required me to accept my powerlessness. I had no control over my mother's choices. I only had control over my own. Her reply served to substantiate the unhealthiness between us, yet I did not regret writing her. It was a necessary part of my journey to inner peace.

Soon thereafter, I made a difficult decision pertaining to my mother. In order to maintain my wholeness, I set a boundary limiting our contact so that I would not be exposed to the triggers that had the potential of collapsing me to someone unrecognizable. As of today, *shared forgiveness* has not occurred between us, though I feel I have achieved *solo forgiveness*. What I learned from this experience is this: not all *unfinished business* has a fairytale ending, but with each attempt to disentangle the past, I am convinced that one's true self becomes clearer.

More than once people have asked me if I wish I had been able to reconcile my relationship with my mother. The answer is an easy, "Yes." The one unremitting truth that hasn't wavered in over twenty years working in mental health is this: every child wants to feel a part of a family. I am no different. The need to belong is an undying thirst and the reason the illusion of *home* in *Christina's World* enticed me so passionately.

Trail Notes

- *Victim* is a fitting term for those negatively affected by their environment; unlike children, adults have a choice in remaining a victim

- Blame is a powerful tool that is best served with *purpose with integrity*

- The *worst case scenario* exercise helps prepare a person for unknown consequences

- Shared forgiveness and solo forgiveness are two options that allow you to move forward less encumbered in life. Forgetting is not possible; reconciliation is a choice

- We are all ordinary people on the trail to finding peace; boundaries help us reach this goal

Chapter Fourteen

Can't Buy Me Peace

Change and the Pursuit of Therapy

Once my stubbornness subsided I reluctantly met with both of the therapy referrals Steven gave me, though I was unable to feel a connection with either of them. The problem, I determined, was they were both women and I was still craving a father. So, as if a child forced to take out the trash, I unenthusiastically opened the phone book, closed my eyes, and randomly let my finger land on the name of a new therapist. Feeling great resentment for having to tell my story yet again, I went to my first appointment with an attitude of, *Prove to me this isn't a waste of my time.* I wanted to scream about how unfair it was to have to go to therapy and spend money I didn't have because other people had messed up my life. But, of course, I didn't. I walked in calmly and reserved knowing I had two sons at home counting on me. In forty years, restraint was one of the few skills I had mastered.

Upon entering Dr. Green's office, my immediate *like* for him generated disappointment. I wasn't prepared for such a smooth transition. A part of me wanted to remain resentful, to find fault with him, to hate him. If I *failed* therapy, after all, that would *show* Steven, right? Yes, my anger had engulfed my logic. But, instead of continuing down this path of resistance, it took only a few moments of Dr. Green's attention to transform my disdain into a little girl's hunger for attention, and therapy resumed where Steven had left off.

A psychiatrist, Dr. Green was a Yale graduate, a university I could only drool over thinking of attending. Undeniably intelligent, I found keeping up with him a welcome challenge. He awoke my desire to want to learn again, to understand, and to heal. And, in time, I even caught myself trusting him. In my desperate pursuit for tranquility, our twice-a-week appointments became the highlight of my life.

As we ventured into my past, however, something unexpected occurred. Dr. Green's questions began triggering a reaction in me similar to that of *tuning out*, as if my thought process became paralyzed, leaving me not only unable to answer his question, but also unable to remember what question he asked. For years I had unknowingly called this feeling *confusion*, but it was more as though my brain was on overload and tripping the circuit breaker, causing everything to turn black. Eventually, I came to realize my brain was attempting to shield me from painful memories. While this reaction no doubt helped protect me in childhood, I was experiencing first-hand how the continued use of a defense mechanism can get in the way of healthy adult functioning. I envisioned the conscious equivalent to that of a child placing his hands over his ears, repeatedly yelling, *I don't hear you!* Yet my reaction initiated without any consent. As a patient, I hated the lack of control I felt. As a budding therapist, however, the brain's propensity to guard against danger fascinated me and I respected that when I was ready to hear them, my memories would unveil themselves.

One of Dr. Green's gifts was relaying enormous amounts of information. Not wanting to miss anything, I went home after each session

CHAPTER FOURTEEN

and wrote down everything I remembered him saying followed by my thoughts that I was yet able to render face-to-face. I then gave Dr. Green my writings at our next meeting, sometimes in excess of five typed pages. Writing allowed me a sense of participation in my otherwise self-restricted observer position. With a deep desire to comprehend everything – and I mean EVERYTHING – I based my ability to heal on understanding why my mind reacted the way it did to my childhood experiences. Not long into therapy, I had no doubt I'd found the right teacher. A session with Dr. Green felt similar to an accelerated course in psychiatry.

Wanting nothing more than to feel *normal,* I set the basis for therapy's termination for when I could go into session and conduct myself as Dr. Green's equal without unwelcome triggers. Week after week, I arrived with anticipation that *today was the day.* As soon as I sat down, however, Dr. Green's mere presence caused me to revert to the emotional immaturity of my strongest void, leaving me both intrigued and ashamed by how quickly I could transgress to that of a child. Dr. Green observed my angst, and a turning point came when he commented on the disparity he saw between the woman who *came to* each session and the woman who *wrote about* our sessions. At last, concrete recognition of the conflict I lived with for as long as I could remember. To the world I may have only been able to show my meek and controlled side, but inside was an inquisitive and vivacious woman longing to escape.

Had I the money, I would have gone to therapy every day. For fifty minutes, Dr. Green granted me safety and a sense of belonging regardless of my presentation. In our short time together, my defenses softened enough to accept another person's help, and even though embarrassed by the thought, I wondered if my feelings compared to that of what a healthy child might feel from a protective father – a sense of security even in the midst of vulnerability.

Eventually I learned my feelings for Dr. Green were called *transference,* a term used when a patient unconsciously redirects feelings about someone else onto their therapist. In my case, I viewed Dr. Green as my father and, as a result, he accrued a fair share of my anger, sadness, and acting out behaviors. While this is what therapy is meant to induce in order to heal root issues, I misinterpreted these feelings as ones that extended beyond patient and therapist. Feeling important, nurtured, cared about, and respected, I knew only that when I was with this warm, funny, smart, and handsome man, my worries dissipated. I felt happy. In turn, these feelings lured me into thinking it was time to leave therapy, a decision that came with one condition I may have failed to communicate candidly to Dr. Green: he needed to remain in my life. In my childish wisdom, I had it all figured out. I didn't need therapy; I needed Dr. Green.

My questionable deduction placed Dr. Green in a position of having to reiterate the ethical boundaries of therapy probably a hundred times. Still, however, I was unable to reconcile his message. My maladapted black and white thinking allowed me to view the situation only as his caring about me or abandoning me. Feeling as though I was reliving my father's disregard for me, my primal needs threatened to collapse my body to the floor, hold on to Dr. Green's pant leg and scream, "Don't leave me! I need you." But my defenses would still not allow such truth. Instead, I aged to a more adolescent gesture, sending the contradictory message, "I don't need you! Show me you care," as if challenging Dr. Green to a duel. In truth, I was neither three nor thirteen, but a forty-year-old woman attempting to compensate for the lack of self-reliance normally achieved when a toddler wanders from her parent to investigate the world, periodically looking back to make sure someone is watching her. In my childhood, this undoubtedly failed to occur successfully. Now, in the midst of the re-creation of this vital childhood developmental stage, I was not able to get one step out of Dr. Green's office before my separation anxiety overtook the rational person I knew was trapped somewhere inside me. I had nightmares about going to my next appointment and finding Dr. Green's office vacant or walking in to discover he didn't recognize who I was. And as much as I understood intellectually that this was my unconscious playing out the deficiencies in my childhood, my faith that this horrific, heart-wrenching emptiness and humiliation would ever go away began to fade.

With patience and skill, Dr. Green supported my often-agonizing journey. He helped me to understand how my experiences affected my present-day life and that just because my father failed to show me consistency and respect, this didn't mean other men would do the same. He allowed me to see how my childhood had resulted in the adoption of some irrational thoughts such as *men would always leave me* and *I was unlovable*. But he also taught me that internal change occurs with external change, as in my behavior. If I was to become the person I believed was stuck inside me, I needed to *act* the part. So, as if a child learning to read, I began practicing new, healthier skills to make up for my compromised development. It was during this part of my journey that I was able to recognize the *real* me emerging.

In the end, it was my choice to conclude therapy, equating it to my long overdue individuation – the excitement yet apprehension an eighteen year old might feel leaving a healthy, happy home for independence. Part of my strength came from knowing Dr. Green, as if a supportive parent, offered to be available for questions or setbacks. My success in therapy gave me proof that missing, damaged, and misplaced puzzle pieces from childhood *can* be found and resolved. This not only signified tribute to Dr. Green's talent and dedication, but also founded the heart of my own counseling career that began soon thereafter.

Envision yourself about to lean on a fence. Just as you touch it, alarming volts of energy run through your body. Realizing the fence is electric, my guess is you quickly move and refrain from leaning on that particular fence again. This is one of the magical aspects of humanness. Input affects output. Your childhood was no different.

🥾 *Exercise 14a: Consider how you feel about change. Do you embrace change or do you avoid change? Think about two examples of change that have occurred in your life, one being a change you chose to make and the other being a change that was made for you. How did you respond to each? How did your feelings differ? Why do you think you reacted the way you did?*

The information in the prior thirteen chapters *can* empower you. By looking at your timeline, you should now be able to see areas requiring your attention in order to achieve a healthier life, including emotional barriers, unresolved relationships, acting out behaviors, developmental voids, stuck defense mechanisms, unprocessed grief, and ineffective communication skills. This chapter focuses on what, if anything, prevents you from utilizing this information and taking advantage of the power available to you. Or, as I prefer to call it: *why you can lead a horse to water but not make him drink*.

Might I first say it is not my intention to *make* you do anything. I am simply supplying the water in case you are thirsty. As you read over the next four scenarios, consider where you are right now on your trail ride.

1) Thirsty: You have thought about what roadblocks stand in your way to a healthier, more powerful life and are ready to face them. You are eager to discover your story, find your missing puzzle pieces, and enjoy the authenticity that will help you acquire your dreams.

2) Thinking about drinking: You are aware you have *guk* in your *guk* bag, but are cautious about opening it up. You wish there was an

easier way, such as a magic pill. You sometimes convince yourself that life is fine the way it is, but deep down you know this to be untrue. You want to start slowly and might need support.

3) Afraid of water: Your fear is overriding your ability to take action. You are questioning the *what ifs* and not feeling confident in your skill level. You know there was unhealthiness in your childhood but are afraid of upsetting the status quo. You need support if you choose to proceed.

4) Not thirsty: Something is blocking your ability to see that your life could benefit from a better understanding of your past. You are hanging on to what you know, trying to convince yourself that everything is fine. Your *truths* remain buried.

One of my favorite quotes is: *The path of least resistance is often a dead end.* In other words, if what you are doing right now hasn't materialized in the achievement of your dreams, it probably won't. Regardless of which category you fall into, I wholly believe in something called *baby steps*. If you saw the movie *What About Bob?* you will remember Bill Murray plays the part of a manipulative, co-dependent, obsessive-compulsive man who follows his psychiatrist on vacation. I watched the movie while in the midst of therapy and, besides making me feel better about my own problems, I also latched on to the fact that I was trying to do too much too soon with regard to changing. You see, I'm not the most patient person you'll ever meet, and when I decide to do something, I want it done already. This movie taught me a skill that has been beneficial in my life both as a fellow human moving toward self-actualization *and* as a therapist supporting other people on their journeys. *Baby steps* is just what it sounds like: making small changes over a period instead of drastic chunks all at once. In fact, I don't recommend anyone begin by making any abrupt or large changes because some adjustments can be overwhelming if your foundation isn't in place. You might be amazed how even one small step has the ability to trickle down and affect many aspects of your life. So, consider beginning with one baby step and see how you feel. Re-reading this book and any of the books from the additional reading section can also be helpful. If you fall into the third or fourth category, you might consider using the *worst case scenario* exercise from chapter thirteen and ask yourself, *what is the worst thing that could happen if I took a baby step?* Utilizing ASSC (awareness, source, solutions, and consequences) can also be helpful. If you find yourself resistant, consider that the roadblock in your way may be disguised *guk* that you need to remove from your trail to authenticity.

There is somewhat of a mystery behind what causes a person to make that first step toward healthy change. If discomfort were enough incentive, our society would be celebrating with *childhood enlightenment parties* because adult stress, anxiety, and depression are at epidemic levels. Since these parties aren't yet the craze, I suspect we need other criteria. In my case, I needed a *goal*. You see, traditional thought is that we should *self-actualize* for ourselves because we are important, great, special, worthy, yada, yada, yada. And while I am not disregarding the significance of self-respect, sometimes – especially if you have been victimized in childhood – a higher level of self-love is needed in order to make it a viable motivating factor. In fact, oftentimes the reason *for* solving problems is to increase one's sense of self-worth. That's why I have found that defining a source outside yourself can be beneficial.

The information I am writing about is what I needed to know when I was emotionally lost and couldn't find help. My deficits originated from what I now refer to as *the perfect childhood storm*: unhealthy norms, complicated attachment, neglect, irrational beliefs, unpreparedness for life, mal-adapted personality, lack of resiliency factors, chronic defense mechanisms, poor communication skills, voids in development, unfulfilled needs, bad decision making, grief, individuation deficits, and prolonged victim status. Lost,

CHAPTER FOURTEEN 219

damaged, and misplaced pieces made up the majority of my puzzle. Simply: layers of *guk* obscured my authentic identity. My *guk* bag wasn't only full, it was overflowing. I was provoked to seek help not because I ever foresaw myself becoming a healthy, happy, whole person, but because I had something in my life that mattered more to me than me: my sons.

🐴. *Exercise 14b: As you look at your timeline and see the big picture of your life, define your reasons for reading this book. Ask yourself what motivates you. What is the goal behind your desire to improve your life? In BIG BOLD LETTERS, write this motivating goal on the top of your timeline. If you want additional support in making changes in your life, design a poster with this motivating goal and hang it where you will see it every day. I covered my refrigerator with pictures of my sons and their artwork.*

So, let's say you decide to resolve some of your losses from your childhood and are making progress on your trail ride when, all of a sudden, you find yourself lost. This is the point where people often ask, "Do I need therapy?" Well, *they say one out of four people admit to needing therapy... and the other three are lying.* Okay, I had to include at least one joke about mental health. But the truth is, it's not that far off base. Being that I am a staunch advocate for self-awareness, I view therapy as simply another tool to help one achieve insight and advance toward self-actualization. So, even though I think most everyone could benefit from self-reflection, here are a few guidelines for when I would highly recommend therapy:

1) If you are having any thoughts to hurt yourself or anyone else, this is a must to seek professional help,

2) If you are having any psychotic symptoms, such as hallucinations, paranoia, or delusions,
3) If you feel out of control and your behavior is negatively affecting your life, or
4) If you are stuck in the process of self-discovery and are not making the process you desire.

Having said that, let's talk about therapy. I tend to look at therapy the same way my horse trainer looks at horses. His business card, in fact, states what he does as: *training, untraining, and retraining*. In therapeutic terms, I alter this to mean *learning, unlearning, and relearning*. This suggests that therapy is preventive, rehabilitative, and proactive, which serves three purposes: to help rectify past experiences, to decrease current unwanted behaviors, *and* to generate a healthier future.

When I searched for a therapist, it was important to me to find someone I felt I could trust with the intimate details of my life. I needed to feel safe so I could speak my truth without feeling further shame. I innately gravitated toward a male therapist because I was still searching for a father figure, a factor that was initially out of my awareness. This connection I'm talking about is one of the first topics I discuss with my new patients. I tell them an important aspect about therapeutic success stems from the rapport between the patient and therapist. I also tell them if, after a couple of sessions, they don't feel we are a good match, I will refer them to someone else. After all, why would anyone follow my advice if they didn't believe I could help them? It's just common sense.

As with most professions, there are both great and not-so-great therapists, plus everything in between. Although it may seem silly, make sure your therapist, or mental health professional, is trained in *how* to conduct therapy. *Therapist* encompasses a wide range of degrees, including therapist, counselor, social worker, psychologist, and psychiatrist, each stemming from varied requirements in graduate school. Some of these programs don't teach the art of therapy. Out of the group listed above, only the psychiatrist is a medical doctor. This also means a therapist's specialty is something worth considering. Similar to doctors, therapists can have general practices or specialize in a particular area, such as substance abuse, marriage counseling, or children. If a therapist is untrained in a particular field, licensure boards consider it unethical for that therapist to practice in that discipline. You wouldn't want a foot doctor performing your open-heart surgery, would you? Also, as with medical doctors, therapists use different methodologies for treatment, charge different fees, and have varied availability, and these topics are worth discussing up-front.

My advice in finding a good fit in a therapist is to narrow your search to three. If you have insurance, it may require you to choose from a particular list of therapists. Otherwise, check your state licensing agency that oversees mental health professionals, your medical doctor, the internet, or ask people you know for referrals. Call the therapists and see if you can talk to each of them for a few minutes. My last two patients grilled me on my education, experience, reason for becoming a therapist, and treatment modalities, and I respected their inquiry.

A traditional therapy session is fifty-minutes in an office setting. Your need and insurance plan, if you have one, help determine frequency of visits. The initial visit should include a discussion on after-hour crisis protocol so you know what to do if an emergency arises. The therapist, an associate, a crisis agency, or 9-1-1 usually attends to these situations.

In my practice, I have found some of the traditional aspects of therapy to have disadvantages. When working with children and their families, I prefer home visits to a sterile office because children tend to be more comfortable in their own environment and are more apt to reenact the concerning behavior. I am also flexible in the length of my sessions, as I don't always find a strict fifty-minute session to be beneficial.

Regardless of setting, style, or cost, it is important to understand that confidentiality laws protect communication in therapy, with a few exceptions. In Arizona, a therapist can break confidentially only if self-harm, harm to others, or abuse to a child or vulnerable adult is thought to exist. Ethical guidelines also found a therapist's work and licensing boards can verify ethical violations against mental health professionals. These laws and guidelines help protect the patient/therapist relationship.

As far as the effectiveness of therapy, research finds the style of therapy is less important than the quality of the relationship between therapist and patient. Therapy modalities include cognitive, behavioral, cognitive-behavioral, gestalt, family-centered, and psychoanalytic, to name a few. I suggest researching different types of therapy for a better understanding of what each is about. This would be no different than deciding between pain management, surgery, or chiropractic adjustments for your back pain treatment. As with medicine, many philosophies exist, and in today's world of vast options, patients need to be their own best advocates by educating themselves prior to making decisions about their bodies.

Regardless of method, the universal goal of quality mental health therapy is finding the truth. Discovering one's truth is pertinent to finding one's authentic self. As a person who doesn't particularly like catch-phrases, the term *authentic self* feels genuine to me. Having lived the majority of my life feeling as if someone else inhabited my body and wanting to scream, "That wasn't me!" in order to defend my behaviors, I find deep meaning and reverence in the expression.

As obviously biased as I am about therapy, it may not be for the reasons you think. I, too, was skeptical of going to a therapist; I wasn't even sure what they did. I had bought into the stigma, the jokes, the craziness it must tell about me. When I finally did go, I had no idea as to all the various techniques possible for helping people solve their problems, of the natural and common issues we all face, of the humanness it represented. Therapy can provide a professional, non-judgmental ear from which to listen, or a surrogate environment where revisiting the past can ensue healing. The beauty of well-delivered therapy is comparable to sitting and watching the

CHAPTER FOURTEEN

most beautiful sunrise as the dark turns to light, ultimately brightening your world. Therapy allows you to experience the natural beauty and power of the human psyche, something medication cannot convey. If discovering your authenticity isn't a journey possible on your own, then having the support of a mental health professional is a true gift.

As much as I know I benefited from therapy, I also realize not everyone needs its intensity. Because of this, I recently added the service of *consulting*. I look at consulting equivalent to a trail guide for individuals who want some one-on-one support as they maneuver through my book. Consulting can also be more convenient than therapy due to its access via the phone or computer. At the request of a patient, I am also developing a weekly teleconference where I share additional information and participants can ask questions and learn from one another. To see more on my services, go to www.childhoodpower.com.

In looking back over all the therapists I have known or experienced, several similarities stand out in the ones I consider to excel in their field. They are open-minded, they have empathy for and insight into human suffering, they are motivated by an intrigue in knowing why people do what they do, they read people well, they are educated, they keep up with advancements, and they don't give up. Unfortunately, this means a person can have twenty degrees and not necessarily be an effective therapist. While knowledge is only one requirement, most of the attributes I described above can't be solely taught in graduate school. These are qualities embedded in a person's soul, and traits of natural healers. When you meet one, you inevitably know. They are drawn to the profession. It is not a job; it is a calling.

The difficulty in explaining the power that therapy plays in self-enlightenment is that it is an overwhelmingly private adventure where no two journeys are the same. The most accurate I have ever been able to describe it was in a poem I wrote for my therapist in an attempt to thank him for giving me back my life.

Tears of Freedom

He appeared belated to my journey, encompassed by an essence of peace,
speaking humbly to my soul
and throwing trust to my temptation.

Who is this man who reaches into my life's abyss and,
with impeccable sagaciousness, pulls out the profound sacrifices of
guilt, and rage, and sadness and shame, yet honors no owned desire?

While I, confronted with the antithesis reflection of my own self-antipathy,
tremble while he compassionately graces my hopelessness and
speaks with intrinsic honesty to each of my sins;
my eyes jealously rendering sightless,
the nakedness lying alien in open view.

Then, as if each secret of my life were a fragile heirloom,
he tenderly embraces and bestows them to his heart,
the remnants of a child's impetuous diffidence –
vigilant to honor time's sanctuary.

And though in contempt of my awe,
I strain in agony to touch this man's dignity toward my childishness,
and I ask him…

"Why?"

"For you breathe," he replies.

And as our eyes virginally embrace,
so do tears of freedom begin to cry down the contour of my being.

My hope is that one day people will embrace *change* more often than dread it, that self-awareness will become the new craze in our society, and that stigma will no longer hinder seeking help for emotional struggles. I will cherish the day people can say, "I'm going to see my therapist" without any more deliberation than if to say, "I'm going to ride my horse."

Trail Notes

- Input affects output; we are products of our environment

- Baby steps help *change* become more manageable

- The level of rapport with your therapist affects success

- Sometimes an entity outside yourself is a powerful reason for change

- Change is easier when you have support

Chapter Fifteen

Sweet Home, Authenticity
Reality and Choices

There were times post-therapy when I felt beaten down by the learning fairy. Having high expectations and limited patience for self-defeat, I envisioned my goals materializing much ahead of their actual arrival. Even with this increased anxiety, however, my blossoming self-awareness enabled me to view the excess energy as the power behind my unrelenting determination instead of a problem needing to be resolved. I would try my best. If I made a mistake, I would try again. Giving up was no longer an option. Freedom was breathing down my neck.

As it is meant to be, therapy provided a controlled environment in which I could safely speak my truth. I was well aware that the real world might not be as kind as Steven or Dr. Green. In preparation, I made a mental checklist to keep me on task. Am I speaking my truth directly and with respect? Am I considering the consequences of my behavior? Does the motive for my actions come from a place of integrity? I equated my agenda to a competitive trail ride where riders must complete certain obstacles if they want to finish successfully. Before I started my journey, I lacked awareness of these requirements. Now I was not only able to recognize barriers to my dreams, but I also had the tools to help me maneuver through them. No longer was my goal figuring out what to change; now my goal was implementing and sustaining the changes I desired. Despite my fortitude, however, doubt lingered that my life would ever transform as I hoped, and each morning I woke with trepidation that the old me had returned. To feel truly free from my *guk* seemed unimaginable.

I was in the midst of *relearning* when I accepted a new job as a supervisor for our county's 24-hour crisis hotline. The allure of crisis work began in graduate school when I volunteered for the fire department's mobile mental health team. Feeling curiously at ease in the midst of turmoil, I came to realize that crises felt *normal* to me. Growing up, I had unknowingly learned to stay calm and observant in chaotic situations in order to remain inconspicuous and safe. The difference as a crisis counselor was that I now had the power to initiate a healthier outcome, and this satisfaction penetrated a place deep in my soul. Each crisis gave me a chance to unveil the truth so that healing could begin, and I couldn't help but wonder if my parents might have benefited from such an intervention.

One of the bonuses of my job was the unlimited opportunities to practice my new communication skills. Receiving over 30,000 calls each month, our security-locked unit of seventy-five crisis phone therapists, dispatchers, and console operators was a venue of controlled chaos, making the ability to focus and think quickly essential skills to possess. One day, while monitoring an emergency call with one ear and listening to the police with the other, the dispatcher interrupted me and challenged these skills. Only seeing her lips move and not understanding what she was asking, I lost focus with both my caller and

CHAPTER FIFTEEN

the police and, pointing to my headphones, non-verbally insinuated, "Can't you tell I'm a little busy here?" Offended, she avoided me for the rest of her shift, causing great tension in the small area we shared for twelve hours. Upon going home and thinking about the incident, I realized how poorly I handled the situation and thought about what I needed to do to rectify our relationship. In the past, I probably would have become defensive and done nothing, allowing the *guk* to build between us. Knowing this wasn't the result I wanted, I apologized to her the next time she worked and told her what I wished I would've done differently. Accepting my apology, our relationship strengthened and, over the next few years whenever we'd find ourselves in the midst of pandemonium, we'd look at each other and crack smiles, thinking back to our prior incident.

Through analyzing incidents such as the one above, I became aware of the behaviors I exhibited that didn't promote the person I wanted to become. Then I worked to improve what wasn't working. That isn't to say I never *acted out* again, but only that now when I messed up I tried to correct my mistakes when they occurred rather than let them grow into something bigger. Not making the same error twice became one of my goals. Before long, I felt the benefit of my efforts through feeling less regret and need to say *I'm sorry*. Eventually, my newly acquired confidence allowed me to walk around the crisis floor with an internal smile, delightfully thinking to myself, *I feel crazy no more*.

My story might have ended here had I not recognized one remaining trigger: my name. I was born *Marjorie Ruth*, a name I had difficulty pronouncing, a name bearing the initials M.R., and a name other children and their parents made fun of due to a singing rhyme wherein Marjorie *kissed the boys and made them cry*. My main aversion to the name, however, grew with my father's distinct pitch as he bribed me so he could get out of the house to go to the bars. "Mar…jorie, do you want to go get some candy?" My body learned to react with a nervous apprehension coupled with an unspoken fury that deemed me vulnerable and powerless. Marjorie was the little girl without a voice. Marjorie was the little girl who grew to hate her unrecognizable self. And, although I felt empathy for her plight, the trigger of the name remained too burdensome for me, even as an adult, to overcome. In the end, I conceded that *Marjorie Ruth* was yet another loss on my journey to freedom.

The idea of changing my name came one day when a crisis employee called to me, "Marji?" Suddenly, a menagerie of disturbing images from my childhood captivated me as contempt rose to my breath, nearly causing me to scream *I'm not Marji!* at the innocent crisis worker. Thus began my quest for a less provoking identifier. For weeks I searched for a new name. When I found the name I liked, I drew the line at my sons' approval. I have always believed my healing should come without cost to them, whether through embarrassment or undesired attention. Without hesitation, however, they supported my endeavor, as well as my name choice. *Ainsley* was adapted from various origins for *in a field*. I, of course, envision the field full of horses. I chose *Grace* because it connects me to my sons, having three letters from each of their names (Gabriel and Zachary). When I hear the word *grace*, I also think of my favorite evening on our East Coast trip when we visited Monhegan Island, an artist colony and fishing village off the coast of Maine. Accessible only by ferry and void of motorized vehicles, we spent most of our time fishing and hiking, though on our final evening the boys played ball with some of the locals. As I watched my sons exert the last of their energy as dusk approached, music from a distant, quaint church lured me to its doors by the most heartfelt rendition of *Amazing Grace* I had ever heard, bringing tears to my eyes. *Grace* continues to hold that power and inspiration for me.

CHAPTER FIFTEEN

On April 11, 2005, I stood in front of a judge as he made my new name official. No longer feeling as though I was a fraud, I spoke my name proudly and distinctly. As a celebration of both closure and a new beginning, I embraced the moment alone, never having believed this day would ever occur in my life: the birth of my true self. Allowing time for adjustment, I officially became Ainsley Grace Collins to the rest of the world on July 4, 2005, my personal independence day.

Babies are born with colossal potential that childhood experiences either propel or stunt. By virtue that *no parent is perfect,* this means the majority of us reach adulthood distanced from our most powerful, authentic selves. Whether we choose to bridge this gap stems from our awareness of its presence, our motivation to live a more conscientious life, and our response to resistance.

I did not turn eighteen and immediately look to my past for answers. My reality was deep in the clutches of an immaturity I might have verbalized as, "Life is good. I'm in love with a great guy and want to get married and have children." With my defenses blocking my insight to the unhealthiness I sustained growing up, I surrendered to society's expectations of a young girl. I had no reason to look backwards. I was deep in denial.

At thirty, reality smacked me in the face. As a divorced, broke, unemployed high school drop-out with two babies in diapers residing in the basement of a friend's home, I viewed myself as a failure – as a wife, provider, woman, and person. Still, I didn't think to look to my past. Instead, my tenacity to hold on to the familiar persevered. My learned survival skills were intact and thriving, leaving little room for reflection. My plight, however, had changed. No longer was I the little girl attempting to endure her environment; I was now a mother safeguarding her children from a similar fate, a position I was willing to die upholding.

By the time I hit forty, I was drowning in the overflow from my *guk* bag. As if a soldier captured by his enemy, I had nowhere to run. Reality forced me to confront my emotional incarceration and invade my childhood memories; therapy became my comrade.

Today my reality is that I have the knowledge and tools to remain healthy if I choose to use them. I view self-actualization as an offering of the human spirit, and inner peace as a reward for valuing the truth. No longer am I ashamed to call myself a *victim*, for I know that the term does not define *who* I am, but what occurred *to* me. This acknowledgement gave me permission to discover my childhood story, find my voice, and gain power over my life. Though not a word I use lightly, I recognize the necessity of *sacrifice* in order to preserve my wholeness. I have come to accept that the cost of internal peace is often the *normalcy* that we relied upon as children.

Ultimately, life is about choices. Our choices can make or break us, open or close doors, enhance or deplete our power, create happiness or cause sorrow. Choices are what we didn't always have as children. We were molded by others' choices – out of love, ignorance, carelessness, ease, or indifference. We lived with each decision, whether healthy or not, adapting and mal-adapting. Some of the choices took a toll on our development, sense of self, and preparedness for life. Most often, the losses stemming from these choices followed us into adulthood, causing us to sustain further deficits. The reality of childhood is this: not every environment is conducive to creating an authentic adult. Neither does a childhood have to be *bad* or *abusive* in order to unveil valuable information. We are products of our experiences; it is only logical that our childhoods hold some of the answers to what ails us.

I remember the first morning I woke up and realized I felt alive. No, I mean A L I V E ! – more than simply a pulsating heart. Eager, fervent, and enthusiastic, I had adjectives describing me that I'm sure had never been used in the same sentence with my name before. My immediate thought as a learned pessimist was to fear this heightened sense of life due to its probable short duration. My budding optimism, however, peeked through and took hold, permitting me to enjoy this incredible new experience that I had forever longed for – genuine, uninhibited happiness.

While elated by the long-awaited change, I realized that letting go of the familiar was not as easy as I envisioned. I struggled with how someone acknowledges forty years of sadness, mistakes, lost dreams, and pain and goes on to accept this beautiful gift of emotional freedom. In what felt like the blink of an eye, the dread I had woken up with almost every day of my life no longer existed. Oh, I looked the same on the outside, but inside I felt real for the first time, perhaps similar to reverse plastic surgery. I wondered if people would notice. Was it as obvious as a boob job or more akin to a tummy tuck? For someone who rarely smiled, would people think it strange that I was happy? Would I look odd smiling? I was ready to find out.

Exercise 15a: It is now time to ask yourself, "Who is my authentic self?" Hint: Discovering this person will take you on a lifelong trail ride where empowerment, pride, peace, and purpose are awaiting you.

This is the point where you begin making choices that create the life you desire. In chapter three I stated you knew how to giddee-up but not how to steer. Well, the reins are now in your hands so you can begin *your* trail ride to genuine, uninhibited happiness. Whether you have minor changes to make or a new identity to create as I did, the choice is now yours. Are you going to remain at the stable or ride into the sunset?

One of the things that helped me when I reached this point on my journey was looking to people I admire for guidance. I knew who I thought I was and wanted to become, but I didn't always know how to get there. Because of this, I sought out people who modeled the characteristics I valued. Nelson Mandela, for example, portrays a humbleness that I revere. Given that I didn't like how I sometimes came across arrogant, he became my role model. Likewise, Ellen DeGeneres became a positive influence in my life due to her ability to enjoy the simple things in life, such as dancing. I started watching her show in my *relearning* phase after I discovered that laughing felt unnatural to me. Having always felt self-conscious displaying joy or happiness, I challenged myself to watch her show. In the beginning, I had to give myself permission to move even discretely to the music. By her second season, I was laughing aloud. Today, my dogs know to move out of the way so I have room to dance, and Fred the basset hound even howls with me when I'm singing along. I urge you to look around and find inspiration from those who can help you aspire to your wholeness.

I imagine by now you recognize that the concepts in this book are not simply a means to understand your past, but a philosophy for living your life. Rarely, if ever, do people stop personal growth after completing their childhood story. Its value is simply without comparison. Those closest to me know I am someone who analyzes everything, and though I have learned to endure being the brunt of related jokes, I offer no apology. Questioning one's beliefs and behaviors is a vital part of the exclusively individual experience that exposes unfeigned humanness. To cease asking how we can improve our emotional well-being would be detrimental to ourselves as well as to our collective society.

🌶. *Exercise 15b: Take a week out of your life and dissect what you do for twenty-four hours a day over seven days. On your timeline, document your feelings, including when you feel stressed, happy, sad, empty, indifferent, energized, passionate, and tired. Identify your routine and pinpoint patterns of behavior. Ultimately, define both what you like and don't like about your life. Think about what you would change regardless of your perceived ability to do so. As you read over the next section, add anything to your timeline that you didn't previously think about.*

After I completed the above exercise, I divided my life into what I call *The Five Areas of Focus* so I could look at how each element contributes to the whole of my happiness. These five areas are:

1) Environment
2) Food, Sleep, and Exercise
3) Fun and Work
4) Relationships and Support
5) Prevention and Purpose

Environment: This category focuses on the geographical location of your home, the climate where you live, your residence, your neighborhood, and your neighbors. Each of these factors affects your stress level in some way, whether positively or negatively, and it is helpful to understand how your environment affects your authentic self. If I described my *perfect environment*, it might sounds like this: a ranch in the boonies on thousands of acres near my sons and their families, friendly supportive neighbors within riding distance but not within sight, warm weather but not too hot, minimal rain, rolling hills with year-around creeks, abundant wildlife that doesn't want to harm me, a

Zach, fourteen, the author, and Gabe, sixteen, on a cattle drive

city within a short distance with everything I need, and a job I could ride to and from on my horse. So, are you getting the picture? This is the environment I envision most ideal for my authentic self. Given that this dream will not likely materialize in my lifetime, my goal is to strive to get as close to it as I can by making conscious choices. About ten years ago, for example, I was able to move into the country and have a little acreage for my horses and a large yard for my dogs. This decision manifested after I took Gabe and Zach on a cattle drive that made me realize how much I missed the freedom and peace of open space, as well as being able to have lots of animals. My current home is not my huge dream ranch, but it's a step closer than my previous residence and I cherish it every day. Although we don't always have the ability or means to change what we don't like about our lifestyle, having an awareness of our likes and dislikes is the first step to knowing what we would change if the opportunity arises. Any option that allows you to design your life more advantageously to your true self benefits your mental health.

CHAPTER FIFTEEN

Food, Sleep, and Exercise: Your eating, sleeping, and exercising habits also affect your emotional health. My body tends to function best if I eat small meals throughout the day rather than two or three larger meals. Over the years I have also become more aware of how *what* I put into my body affects *how* I feel. I now lean toward vegetarianism for a couple of reasons: my love of animals, and I simply feel better. Likewise, I have a need for about eight hours of sleep on a consistent schedule. If I stay up too late or don't get enough sleep, I end up feeling as though I have a hangover in the morning, a consequence I don't particularly enjoy. As far as physical activity, my exercising habits have actually improved with age. Although I have never been one who enjoys forced movement such as aerobics or lifting weights, I love feeling fit. An added bonus is that the more I exercise, the more I can eat. I hike four mornings a week, ride my horses every chance I get, and there are always chores waiting for me.

Fun and Work: Little compares to feeling good about what you do. Fun, laughter, and positive thoughts promote healthiness. If you don't laugh at least once a day, ask yourself why. Doing what you enjoy nourishes your soul. I have animals because they not only allow me to feel a connectedness to other living creatures, but they also bring me joy. Nothing makes me smile more than coming home and having Fred the basset hound follow me around the house *talking* to me about his need for food. My four other dogs, as well, each amuse me with their individual quirks. Some would say my dogs dictate my life, but it works for me.

The best means for limiting stress at work is to have passion for what you do. People who are able to combine what they love with how they earn a living are usually happier individuals. When you enjoy a task, stress ceases to be a negative factor. If your work cannot be that venue, consider a hobby or volunteering at something you would choose as your dream job. If what you do also benefits society in some way, I applaud you. Improving the greater healthy good is a proven remedy for enhancing one's mental outlook.

Relationships and Support: Belonging is a human need that never goes away. Having people you can count on to healthily support you in life is magical. The stress caused from loneliness and unhealthy relationships is, literally, sickening. Relationships are what allow us to reflect on our own behavior, and that's why I want people around me who I can trust to be honest with me. I like the idea of someone caring enough to speak up if they think I am making a bad decision. Sometimes these people are family. Other times they are people we choose to be our *family*. Either way, they provide nourishment for our mental health.

Prevention and Purpose: I am an avid promoter of preventive measures. The four preceding categories are just that: areas where the choices you make either prevent or create emotional distress in your life. Another preventive measure is holistic medicine. Looking at your mind and body as interacting parts is advantageous for maintaining optimum health. Finding specialists to support you in this goal is critical as well. I visit my doctor, various specialty doctors, my dentist, my massage therapist, and my chiropractor as needed. Their expertise helps me stay as healthy as possible. This is important to me because I intend on riding horses well into my nineties. I have to make up for lost time, after all.

If I had to choose one life-encompassing factor, however, it would be *purpose*. When you feel purpose for what you do with your life, a kind of inner bulldozer plows through anything that gets in your way. I have been fortunate to feel more than one purpose in my life: mothering (both my children and my animals) and helping others find inner peace. For me, purpose begins deep in my soul, and stopping it is not an option. Mohandas Gandhi displayed purpose in non-violence; Mother Teresa did so combating poverty and hunger. Understanding yourself and choosing not to waste energy on battling internal conflicts allows you the opportunity to feel a purpose that helps to create a more humane world. If you don't know yours already, I believe your purpose will be waiting for you as your authenticity reveals itself.

🥾 *Exercise 15c: On your timeline, describe what your 'perfect environment' looks like. Now, let this ideal guide you on your trail ride to your dreams.*

Congratulations! You're almost there. Just a couple more paragraphs and you will officially be ready to begin your trail ride. You have now read the groundwork needed for success. My advice is to go at your own pace and carefully prepare for how you want to respond to each obstacle you encounter. There is also a reading list at the end of this book if you desire additional information, as well as a list of all the questions you answered throughout this book for easy reference. I welcome feedback and am available for support and guidance if needed. To contact me or find out about my services, go to my website at www.childhoodpower.com.

So, let me be the first to say, "Happy trails!"

And now, a few parting words…

It was with great sorrow that I listened to the tape of Michael Jackson's last words. Speaking in a poignant and tender tone, he grieved of not having a childhood. To think that such a famous, beloved, talented, and wealthy man in our country summed up his life in this way is telling of the significance our childhoods play in our lives. And although it appeared he felt alone, reality would confirm he was not. Celebrities, politicians, family members, friends, neighbors, and convicts alike speak of their troubled pasts, substantiating that unhealthy childhoods are at an epidemic proportion, unprejudiced by socioeconomic class, race, religion, and education level.

At the end of the day, there is no one harder to live with than a false self, making the puzzle of one's life perhaps the most dignified of aspirations. Without honest exploration and resolution of childhood losses and voids, life can have a disheartening outcome. And while I've yet to fully understand why some people choose to pass up the opportunity to embrace their childhood story, I revel in knowing that those who do will be humbled in its delight.

Epilogue

In the end, I consider myself fortunate. Like many others, I was a victim of an alcoholic household. Doused with chronic emotional abandonment, I surrendered to seclusion in order to avoid what my developing mind was incapable of comprehending. The consequences of these experiences have ruled my life. Through the epitome of humanness, my therapists guided me to new understanding. Today I cherish my second chance, no longer waking to apathy, but to an eagerness to begin my day. Of momentous value to me are my family and friends for their love and support, my dogs for their unprecedented devotion, my patients who graciously allow me to be a part of their journey to insightfulness and, of course, all horses, for founding the sustenance of my existence. Such reward sustains both the purpose and meaning to my life.

Additional Reading

Black, Claudia, *Changing Courses,* Denver: MAC Publishing, 1993.

Burchard, Brendon, *The Charge,* New York: Free Press, 2012.

Cain, Susan, *Quiet: The Power of Introverts in a World that Can't Stop Talking,* New York: Random House, Inc., 2012.

Covey, Stephen R., *The 7 Habits of Highly Effective Families*, New York: Golden Books, 1997.

Covey, Stephen R., *The 7 Habits of Highly Effective People*, New York: Free Press, 1989.

Friel, John and Friel, Linda, *An Adult Child's Guide to What's "Normal"*, Florida: Health Communications Inc., 1990.

Goleman, Daniel, *Emotional Intelligence,* New York: Bantam Books, 1995.

Heath, Chip and Heath, Dan, *Switch: How to Change Things When Change is Hard,* New York: Random House, Inc., 2010.

Herman, Judith, *Trauma and Recovery*, New York: Basic Books, 1992.

Hurson, Tim, *Think Better*, New York: The McGraw-Hill Companies, 2008.

Johnson, Spencer, *Who Moved My Cheese?,* New York: Penguin Putnam, Inc., 1998.

Kalas, Steven C., *Human Matters,* Nevada: Stephens Press LLC, 2008.

Karen, Robert, *Becoming Attached*, Oxford: Oxford University Press, 1994.

Kubler-Ross, Elisabeth, and Kessler, David, *On Grief and Grieving: Finding the Meaning of Grief Through the Five States of Loss,* New York: Scribner, 2005.

Laney, Marti Olsen, *The Introvert Advantage; How to Thrive in an Extrovert World*, New York: Workman Publishing Company, Inc., 2002.

McKay, Matthew, and Davis, Martha, *Messages: The Communication Skill Book*, California: New Harbinger, 2009.

Miller, Alice, *The Truth Will Set You Free*, New York: Basic Books, 2001.

Maurer, Robert, *One Small Step Can Change your Life,* New York: Workman Publishing Co. Inc., 2004.

Nichols, Michael P., *No Place to Hide*, New York: Prometheus Books, 1995.

Pausch, Randy, *The Last Lecture,* New York: Hyperion, 2008.

Peck, M. Scott, *The Road Less Traveled*, New York: Touchstone, 1978.

Schaefer, Charles E., and DiGeronimo, Theresa Foy, *Ages & Stages: A Parent's Guide to Normal Childhood Development,* New York: John Wiley & Sons Inc., 2000.

Schreiber, Flora Rheta, *Sybil*, New York: Warner Books, 1973.

Tieger, Paul D. and Barron-Tieger, Barbara, *Do What You Are*, New York: Little, Brown and Company, 1992.

Viorst, Judith, *Necessary Losses*, New York: Fireside, 1986.

Whitfield, Charles L., *Healing the Child Within*, Florida: Health Communications Inc., 1987.

Exercises

- *Exercise 1a: Take a moment and think about three or four words that describe your overall childhood experience and write them on your timeline. This is your first step to achieving a healthier and more fulfilling life.*

- *Exercise 1b: Close your eyes and envision your first memory. How old are you? Where are you? What are the circumstances? How is this memory significant to you? When you are finished with this memory, try to think of your second memory. Write these down on your timeline at the age they occurred.*

- *Exercise 1c: How would you answer the question, "Who am I?" Begin by writing down six characteristics that define who you are right now. In other words, if you were writing a novel and you were the main character, how would you describe yourself so the reader would feel as though they know your personality? Because we are all human, try to think of three positive characteristics and three characteristics that you would like to improve upon.*

- *Exercise 2a: "If you knew your life would benefit, what would stop you from exploring your childhood?" Write your answer on your timeline.*

- *Exercise 2b: Think of as many emotions as you can and write them on your timeline. Then, next to each emotion, write down a short statement defining how you generally respond to that emotion. For example, next to "joy", I would write "smile".*

🥾 *Exercise 3a: If you wrote a job description for parents, what would it say? Add this to your timeline.*

🥾 *Exercise 3b: As you consider your beliefs about parenting, think about where your beliefs originated. Do they stem from your parents? A friend? An expert? Something you read? Add your answers to your timeline.*

🥾 *Exercise 3c: You will use this exercise throughout your trail ride to discover your childhood story. I call it "Processing a Story" (PAS) and there are five easy steps:*
1) *Choose an experience from your childhood and think about everything that occurred.*
2) *Limit everything you thought about to only facts. (I find this exercise easiest if I pretend I'm reading a screenplay. In looking at the scenario where the police arrested my father, for example, it might sound like this: A father is driving down the road intoxicated with a gun in the car when a lit-up police car approaches. The father pulls off the road and stops. A young child crawls into the back seat and hides.) You are simply telling the story without judgment or emotion.*
3) *Now consider the healthiness of your experience. (In my story, for example, one of the areas of concern is the fact that a young child is riding in a car with an intoxicated person. Another area of concern would be the gun in the car.)*
4) *Visualize the scenario again, this time paying attention to your body's reaction and what you felt. Try to remember both your positive and negative feelings at the time of the experience. For me, it helps to close my eyes and visualize the event when I do this.*
5) *Lastly, consider the impact of this experience on you. Did your worldview change? Did any of your beliefs or behaviors change?*

Was any emotion left unresolved? What was the outcome of the experience?

Exercise 3d: In exercise 1c, I asked you to think about six characteristics that describe who you are. Now ask two friends you trust to do the same in regards to you, three positive characteristics and three characteristics they view would benefit from improvement. Sometimes it is difficult for us to see certain aspects of ourselves. The more honest your friends are, the more helpful the information will be for you. Write their responses next to yours on your timeline. As you compare your self-assessed characteristics to those your friends gave you, consider the similarities and differences. If you aren't clear about or disagree with a characteristic given to you by one of your friends, ask for examples. Try to see yourself through their eyes. Becoming aware of how other people view us is of great value in being better able to understand ourselves.

Exercise 4a: Think of five goals that would improve your life and write them on your timeline. Next to each goal, write down any roadblock(s) that stand in your way of achieving that goal. In other words, why haven't you already accomplished these goals?

Exercise 4b: Think of any childhood intrusions you experienced growing up and add them to your timeline at the age they occurred.

Exercise 4c: Given the definitions of healthy, dysfunctional, abusive, and childhood intrusions, how would you describe your childhood? This will be your baseline definition. I might have described my baseline as "healthy with some possible dysfunction" had I described it before therapy. The reason for this is that I did not yet understand the difference between normal and healthy. I, like many people, did not correlate the cause of my adult problems as having originated in childhood. I also did not realize the truths of my childhood yet, so many of my beliefs were faulty. Today I describe my childhood as "mostly dysfunctional with some abuse and a few intrusions" when I am asked.

Exercise 4d: Read the characteristics of healthy, dysfunctional, and abusive families again. Now, pretend you are a stranger walking into your house when you were a child. Choose a memorable day. Apply PAS (processing a story) from chapter three. What did you learn?

Exercise 5a: Think of a time you acted out. What were the circumstances? What did you do? Try to remember how you felt. What was the outcome? Write a short summary on your timeline.

Exercise 5b: Before moving on, think of as many 'acting out' scenarios as you can remember from your childhood and add them to your timeline at the approximate age they occurred. As you think of more over time, add them as well.

Exercise 5c: As you read about different childhood needs in the next few chapters, go back to your list of acting out incidents and see if you can define the missing need. In other words, why were you acting out?

Exercise 5d: Consider what you would do if you were five years old, hungry, and had no one to give you food. Come up with at least five options you might try in order to avoid starvation.

Exercise 5e: Envision yourself from birth to five years old. I realize I pick on this age, but it's due to my love for kindergartners. They have a certain combination of innocence, intrigue, and adventure about life that would probably do us all good to remember. So, here we go. Picture the setting where you were born. Think of the home or homes you have lived in, the city or cities, birthdays, holidays, special events, your siblings, friends, and relatives, pre-school, and kindergarten if you attended. Who was your caregiver(s)? What do you look like? Describe yourself, your interests, and your talents. Summarize this information and add it to your timeline.

- *Exercise 6a: Take a few minutes to write down Maslow's five levels of needs on your timeline.*

- *Exercise 6b: Add Erikson's stages to your timeline for easy reference. These, along with Maslow's five levels of needs from exercise 6a, will help you to see the bigger picture of development as well as how these theories complement each other in child development.*

- *Exercise 7a: Write down the four characteristics of your temperament. For example, I am an introvert, a morning person, a kinesthetic/visual learner, my interests include horseback riding, animals, classical music, and human behavior, and two of my talents are making cinnamon rolls and scrapbooking.*

- *Exercise 7b: Think about all the different personality traits you have had over the years and add them to your timeline at the approximate age you remember them. On my timeline, for example, I placed traits such as shy and quiet in my preschool area, then added devious and manipulative during grade school, depressed and suicidal in junior high school, impulsive and impatient with a hopeful optimism when I met Brian, and so on, showing both the range of traits I remember having as well as the traits I was labeled by others.*

🐾 *Exercise 8a: As you think about the defense mechanisms discussed in this chapter, consider if you have experienced any of them and place them on your timeline at the age you think they developed. As with any of the previous exercises, you can continue adding to your timeline as your awareness broadens.*

🐾 *Exercise 8b: Think about the last disagreement or argument you had with someone. Take this incident and use PAS (processing a story) from exercise 3c. Now, think of two additional disagreements or arguments and do the same. How did you respond in each of the situations? Do you see any patterns in your action or non-action? Arguments often provide an example of when we use a defense mechanism because emotions are high and the majority of people don't like conflict, so our defenses tend to engage. Most people also find a pattern in their behavior when it comes to conflict. Was the conflict resolved in the situations you assessed? Did you use any defense mechanisms? Do you foresee the same type of conflict arising again? Keep in mind that defense mechanisms often interfere with healthy resolution.*

🐾 *Exercise 8c: Make a list of both your positive and negative triggers and write them on your timeline. Add additional triggers as they come into your awareness.*

🐾 *Exercise 8d: What resiliency factors did you have growing up that added to your sense of belonging, hope, and power? These factors can be people, pets, places, goals, or experiences (school, hobbies, jobs, sports). Did you have at least one adult on whom you could count? Add these to your timeline.*

🥾 *Exercise 9a: If you had to summarize your current relationship with your parent(s), what would you say? Write your answer to this question on your timeline.*

🥾 *Exercise 9b: Consider how you prepared for adulthood. Did your parents talk to you about what it meant to become an adult? What lessons were presented to you? Did you know what was expected of you as you turned eighteen? Did you attend any type of ritual? Did you consider turning eighteen as an event that added responsibility to your life? Write your thoughts on your timeline.*

🥾 *Exercise 9c: Out of 'The Nine Necessities', write the ones on your timeline that you think you needed more education about in preparing for adulthood. How did the absence of this knowledge affect you as an adult? Have you since attempted to gain information on the topic?*

🥾 *Exercise 9d: In exercise 4a you listed the roadblocks that stood in the way of five of your life's goals. Now consider in which of 'The Nine Necessities' categories each roadblock belongs and add it to your timeline.*

🥾 *Exercise 9e: When you make a decision, do you ever feel you need your parents' permission? Are you ever afraid to tell your parents something because you fear their response? When do you feel empowered in your relationship with your parents? When do you feel uncomfortable in your relationship with your parents? When you are with your parents, do you act like an adult or do you revert to child-like behaviors? Do you ever feel as though your parents still have child-like expectations of you? If your parents are deceased, these questions can still be helpful. Just because our parents may not be living does not mean they cease to have power over us.*

🥾 *Exercise 9f: Have you defined any past unhealthiness pertaining to your parents? If "yes", has the issue(s) been resolved? If not, what is the roadblock? Summarize your thoughts on your timeline.*

🥾 *Exercise 9g: If you wrote a job description for children, what would it say? Add this to your timeline.*

🥾 *Exercise 9h: What, if anything, do you think children owe their parents? Write your answer on your timeline.*

🥾 *Exercise 10a: Think about any losses you remember from your childhood and write them on your timeline at the age they occurred.*

🥾 *Exercise 10b: Now that we have defined different types of losses, think back over your childhood and add any other losses you remember. Then next to each loss, write down what type of loss it represents (physical, need, experience, life skill, or expectation, hope, or dream). As you continue your trail ride, add additional losses and type as you identify them.*

🥾 *Exercise 10c: On your timeline, label each of your losses as primary or secondary. Now look for any correlations between your acting out behaviors, your personality characteristics, your defense mechanisms, and any childhood invasions. Where do any concerning areas fall in relation to the theories of Maslow and Erikson? Questioning associations is helpful. When I look at my early teenage years on my timeline and see that I overdosed on pain pills, for example, I ask "Why?" When I answer, "Because I felt lonely and hopeless," I again ask "Why?" This eventually leads me to my feeling unloved by my father, which is shown on my timeline by some of my early experiences with him. Discovering primary losses is a process. Keep in mind we feel and behave certain ways for particular reasons and those reasons are important to understand so resolution can occur.*

- *Exercise 10d: How did you learn about grieving? How did each of your parents grieve? Looking at each of the losses on your timeline, write down the way(s) in which you responded to each loss. Circle each loss you feel you are still grieving.*

- *Exercise 10e: Going back to the losses on your timeline, consider what void or voids developed and, using the list above, write the void and category beside the loss. An example in my life was the loss of a responsible father figure (a need), and this resulted in voids in all the categories, though a few examples are safety (developmental stage), feeling part of a family (relationship), having my father walk me down the aisle at my wedding (event), as well as knowledge and numerous skills one would expect a father to teach his child.*

- *Exercise 11a: Choose one or two of the losses/voids from your timeline and consider which method of healing you might utilize. Give some thought to how you might proceed but do not begin the process. Some of the information yet to come will help you achieve the healthiest outcome. The action part of this entire process comes after information gathering and enhancing self-awareness as mentioned early-on in this book.*

- *Exercise 11b: Write down five solutions to the following problem: While shopping, you think you see your best friend's sixteen-year-old son who has recently joined a gang put a store item in his pocket. As he does this, you think you also see a gun. What do you do?*

Exercise 11c: Given the five options you considered, weigh the possible consequences. How might each choice change your life, your relationship with your friend, your safety, or your emotional health? Did any of your choices tempt you to act against your values, morals, or beliefs? Which option did you choose and why?

Exercise 12a: How would you describe your communication style? What method of communicating do you prefer best: talking, writing, face-to-face, telephone, email, texting, or Skype? Why? What is your least favorite? Again, why? Consider any feedback you receive when communicating, whether it is "you're a good listener" to "please don't interrupt me" to "say something!" In a typical month, how often do you resort to silence in order to avoid perceived confrontation and how often do you yell in order to get your point across? Do you ever regret any of the things you say?

Exercise 12b: Consider the following scenario: Your best friend promises to bring dessert for an important gathering you are having, but then doesn't show up and doesn't bother to call you. Later you run into her at the grocery store. How do you think you would feel? What do you think you would say to her?

Exercise 12c: Think back to the last exercise and to what you decided to say to your friend. Now, assess whether you used the three rules of communication (HRD). If not, see if you can re-phrase your statement using HRD. Try to imagine yourself as your friend and feel the difference in the two responses. If you have had any conversations in the recent past that have not gone well, think about how you might have communicated differently using HRD. From this point on, try to incorporate HRD into your life. My experience has been that you won't be sorry.

🥾 *Exercise 13a: When you hear the word "victim", what is your first thought? How would you define the word? Write down your answers on your timeline.*

🥾 *Exercise 13b: Look at the losses on your timeline and underline any you consider your fault. Next to each of these, write a short statement explaining why you think you are blameworthy.*

🥾 *Exercise 13c: Have you ever faced any difficult past truths? What were some of the consequences of your experiences? Are you aware of any past truths that you are ignoring? Do any of them feel like secrets? If so, consider adding these to your guk bag.*

🥾 *Exercise 13d: In exercise 13b you underlined the losses you thought were your fault. Return to these and consider if anyone could've prevented these losses. My losses, for example, stemmed from my unhealthy experiences with my father. For quite some time I blamed myself for these. I believed I was the wrong gender, not likeable, and a burden. As I looked at my childhood using PAS (processing a story), however, I realized that it was not my job as a child to understand and compensate for my father's shortcomings. I then questioned who could have prevented these losses, or who was ultimately responsible. I came up with two people: my father and my mother.*

🥾 *Exercise 13e: What are your beliefs regarding forgiveness? What is forgiveness? What does healthy forgiveness look like? What is the goal of forgiveness? Add these answers to your timeline.*

🥾 *Exercise 14a: Consider how you feel about change. Do you embrace change or do you avoid change? Think about two examples of change that have occurred in your life, one being a change you chose to make and the other being a change that was made for you. How did you respond to each? How did your feelings differ? Why do you think you reacted the way you did?*

🥾 *Exercise 14b: As you look at your timeline and see the big picture of your life, define your reasons for reading this book. Ask yourself what motivates you. What is the goal behind your desire to improve your life? In BIG BOLD LETTERS, write this motivating goal on the top of your timeline. If you want additional support in making changes in your life, design a poster with this motivating goal and hang it where you will see it every day. I covered my refrigerator with pictures of my sons and their artwork.*

🥾 *Exercise 15a: It is now time to ask yourself, "Who is my authentic self?" Hint: Discovering this person will take you on a lifelong trail ride where empowerment, pride, peace, and purpose are awaiting you.*

🥾 *Exercise 15b: Take a week out of your life and dissect what you do for twenty-four hours a day over seven days. On your timeline, document your feelings, including when you feel stressed, happy, sad, empty, indifferent, energized, passionate, and tired. Identify your routine and pinpoint patterns of behavior. Ultimately, define both what you like and don't like about your life. Think about what you would change regardless of your perceived ability to do so. As you read over the next section, add anything to your timeline that you didn't previously think about.*

🥾 *Exercise 15c: On your timeline, describe what your 'perfect environment' looks like. Now, let this ideal guide you on your trail ride to your dreams.*

www.ingramcontent.com/pod-product-compliance
Lightning Source LLC
Chambersburg PA
CBHW062154080426
42734CB00010B/1685